NEW ENGLAND PLANTATIONS

Commerce and Slavery

D1572040

ROBERT A. GEAKE

THE
History
PRESS

Published by The History Press
Charleston, SC
www.historypress.com

First published 2021

Manufactured in the United States

ISBN 9781467148146

Library of Congress Control Number: 2020951995

In loving memory of Barbara Louise Kenney Geake
1916–1960

CONTENTS

ACKNOWLEDGEMENTS

The germ of this book began with the completion of my history of the Providence River in 2014. In the course of researching material for that history, I found much more than I had known before of the ties to slavery shared within many Rhode Island communities.

I was also employed at Brown University and had, in the years I worked there, met a number of the young scholars who were researching the subject. My acquaintance with them and the opportunity to attend lectures and panel discussions on campus gave me an understanding of the profound reach of slavery into our world and the subsequent effect on the souls of those nations involved, including our own. This reach still extends into many of our own communities, as this book reveals.

Those scholars include Philip Gould, Linford Fisher and Seth Rockman of the Brown University History Department whose works are mentioned within this narrative. Other staff, friends and members of the John Carter Brown Library at Brown University have also provided support over the years, including former director Ted Widmer and present director Neil Safire, as well as the numerous friends of the library who have supported my work. I am especially indebted to the library's commitment to digitizing their image collection, portions of which grace these pages.

I would also like to thank Christian McBurney, an authority on the Narragansett planters; Charlotte Carrington-Farmer, associate professor of history at Roger Williams College for her perspectives, especially on the Narragansett Pacer; and Joe McGill of the Slave Dwelling Project, whom I hosted, along with students from Salve Regina College, at an overnight stay in Smith's Castle.

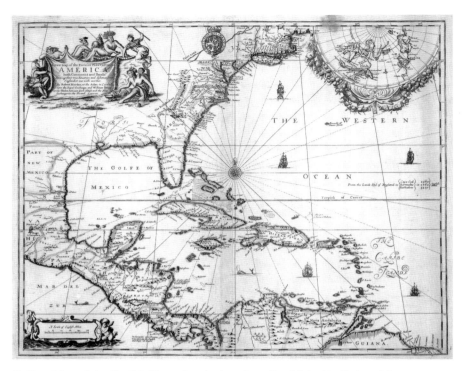

"A New Map of the English Plantations in America…" published by Robert Morton, London, 1673. *Courtesy of the John Carter Brown Library at Brown University.*

I would like to thank the librarians and staff of the Robinson Research Library for their patience in deciphering my request cards and for their help in navigating the collections of the Rhode Island Historical Society. In addition, I would like to thank Mike Kinsella of The History Press and my editor Abigail Fleming for her work on the manuscript.

I would also like to thank the staffs of the Prudence Crandall Museum in Canterbury, Connecticut, and the Center for the Study of Slavery and Justice at Brown University, who hosted a presentation from this work in progress. As with all my work, I hope this book will be a bridge to those academic writings that may provide greater detail on aspects of the subject than can be presented in a work of popular history such as this. To that end, I also hope readers will avail themselves of the bibliography provided. All language and spelling from letters, diaries and logbooks has been preserved for this narrative.

Parts of this manuscript were also published on the blog smallstatebighistory.com

PROLOGUE

Historically, the term *plantation* was used to describe a large piece of land used for commercial purposes, an early example being the Roman latifundia, on which the labor of slaves produced great quantities of wine and olive oil for the empire to export. With the growth of British expansion and colonialism, the term became something else, commonly used to denote a settlement of people who traveled from one place and established a plantation for exporting the resources culled from the new land.

Great Britain first began this experiment during the Tudor reign of the sixteenth century with the move to Anglicize Ireland by confiscating lands and colonizing the counties with elite Protestant landowners. The original form of an "exemplary plantation" involved settling a small colony of Englishmen that would provide a model farming community for the Irish to emulate. But when this plan largely failed, lands were confiscated for more English plantations. A succession of rebellions in the late sixteenth century gave more land to the English, and those members of Irish clans involved who were not killed were held as captive laborers.

The same pattern would show itself in the colonies of British North America. An early effort by the Virginia Company to establish a settlement in Maine failed after just a few months. The settlement in Jamestown took years to become productive. Speculators in England had become wary, though they supported numerous voyages that included Puritan dissidents, unwanted troublemakers and unclaimed or indigent children used as "gifts" for the indigenous rulers encountered for trade, as well as wayward men desperate for a second chance in a new land.

The plantations at Plymouth famously struggled initially, with the Pilgrims losing half their number that first winter and spring of 1620. Those who followed aboard the *Fortune* the following year fared poorly as well. Ill equipped to farm, let alone in New England, they bought goods from the indigenous people and lay low during the bounty of summer, much to the chagrin of William Bradford. As winter came on, some began to starve to death and kept themselves in a stupor with drink. Others indentured themselves to nearby natives for want of food and clothing. The influence of the militant Myles Standish turned things in the favor of future European investors, but only for a time. The economic downturn in the late 1630s affected all trade from New England, leading settlers to turn away from sole agricultural endeavors.

John Winthrop wrote from Boston that the difficult times "set our people on work to provide fish, clapboards, plank, etc. and to sew hemp and flax (which prospered very well) and to look out to the West Indies for trade."[1]

Thus the settlement there opened trade with Barbados and other islands. In exchange for cattle and provisions sent from Massachusetts, the colony received goods such as sugar, tobacco, cotton and indigo. These goods were in turn sold for much-needed cash, which proved to be "a good help to discharge our debts in England."[2]

In 1638, some 250 people—men, women, children and servants—arrived at Quinnipiac Bay to settle the colony of New Haven in what would eventually become Connecticut. Among them was a Black woman named Lucretia, a slave of Theophilus Eaton, who would become the first governor of the colony.

That same year, the fledgling settlement of Providence, just two years after its humble beginnings, was sending hogs and corn to join the trade from Boston. The town of Portsmouth managed to make up a cargo of bolts, clapboards, pipe staves, planks and shooks for the Barbados planters' housing in 1640.[3]

Rhode Island and Providence Plantations, as the colony came to be called, held an unusual position among her sister colonies—being the first established by an exiled puritan minister. Roger Williams, the rogue minister who had left Boston, then was exiled from Salem, Massachusetts, founded the colony on the premise of "Liberty of Conscience," or the freedom to hold one's own political and religious beliefs without punishment from the colony's civil authority; so long as one took a role in civic responsibilities. This separation of church and state would become one of the hallmarks of the nation's founding, but in 1636, the radical views that Williams and his followers held were considered dangerous and a threat to the Puritan laws controlling those subjects of Massachusetts Bay and Connecticut.

Looking at this small colony gives us a unique view into the development of what would be the most lucrative plantation economy in New England. For a time the northern plantations paralleled their southern counterparts, which would eclipse them by the nineteenth century.

Roger Williams and his followers believed that such "a civill state" could exist in such a wilderness and that bonds of friendship and trade with the indigenous people would lead to a coaligned trust and prosperity for those early settlers. As Williams journeyed to London in 1643 for the "patent of civil incorporation" for the colony, he composed *A Key into the Language of America*; a tract that was part travelogue, part foreign-language dictionary, but mostly an invitation for those men of a more adventurous sort-hunters and trappers, as well as speculators to come and trade with the indigenous people of the region. While Williams would realize his vision of a civil state ruled by and with laws created by its citizens, the hope of a prolonged peace and trust between indigenous tribes and European settlers never truly materialized. Such a civil state naturally attracted many who were rebuffed or persecuted by the old Puritan laws still enforced in neighboring colonies.

Rhode Island soon became known for its "loose and degenerate practices." One official in New Amsterdam wrote that the colony "is the receptacle of all the riff-raff people and is nothing else but the sewer latrina of New England.…[A]ll the cranks of New England retire thither."[4]

When charged years after its founding that he had garnered the best lands for his own use and wealth, Williams insisted that when lands were first divided in Providence, he had resolved to receive "only unto myself one single share, equal unto any of the rest of that number."

His first venture after the founding of Providence was the purchase of Chibachuwese Island, a three-thousand-acre island in the Upper Bay. The Narragansett sachem Canonicus offered the island to Williams and John Winthrop for the purpose of keeping their swine and other livestock. The pair purchased the land in 1638 and renamed it Prudence Island, then bought two smaller islands nearby, christening them Patience and Hope.

Cocumscussoc, whose place names includes the Algonquian description of "place of marshy meadows," was the site allocated to Williams for a trading house. He later testified that "Canonicus Laid me out bounds for a trading house at Nahigansett with his own hands, but he never traded with me but has truly what he desired, goods and money…and my trading house which yielded me a hundred pound profit per annum.…God knows that for the public peace-sake I left and lost it about 20 years since when I went last to England."[5]

It is estimated that Williams lived and actively engaged in business at his trading house for twelve years and lived there during the trading season for at least eight of them. Williams envisioned that the trading post he built at Cocumscussoc would be the hub of commerce, negotiation and news brought into the colony. In many respects he was right, but by the 1660s, Williams was also distancing himself from the constant quarrels over land and boundaries and the resulting bitterness and mistrust that grew between the towns of the small colony.

Historian Bruce C. Daniels noted, "Fights over land also fueled many of the internal town struggles; Providence's, the most spectacular, lasted well beyond 1663 and centered on who owned the common land."[6] At a town meeting, the perplexed council, unable to quell dissensions, wrote into the record that they implored the inhabitants to "heal the sores in this town… which do arise about land."

Of the colony's three other towns, Warwick would see part of its holdings temporarily confiscated by Massachusetts. Not formally part of the original incorporation, Warwick found itself left aligned with Providence after 1644 when William Coddington attempted to divide the colony, obtaining a brief appointment as "governor for life" of Newport and Conanicut Island in 1651.[7]

Portsmouth residents overcame efforts in 1644 and again in 1652 by the original purchasers, or "disposers," to claim exclusive rights to "lay out and assign the common land." The town meeting rejected these claims, ruling that land within the town "shall be bounded common to the inhabitants of this town…and land was not to be disposed of without the consent of all the inhabitants."[8]

Those first purchasers had divided huge tracts of land among themselves, and little was left for new arrivals, even while much of the land owned by the "disposers" went unused and unimproved. Eventually, a compromise was reached where these early settlers deeded some land back to the town for dispersal. This led to more tensions, however, as word of the available land led to a flood of new settlers. Daniels wrote, "Not only did successive waves of new arrivals fight over control of land policy, but 'serious debates and agitations' occurred when neighbor fought neighbor over boundaries."[9]

As for Newport, whose interests were largely maritime, the town disputed the boundary on Aquidneck Island with neighboring Portsmouth for so long that the conflict did not end until Charter of 1663, when the General Assembly finally ordered them to cease and desist.

The division of the colony forced by Coddington's ambitions prompted the freemen of Providence Plantations to prevail on Roger Williams to return to England and get Coddington's appointment revoked. Williams relented, in spite of facing much personal loss. As Rhode Islander Bertram Lippincott wrote, "Never wealthy, he sold his land at Cocumscussoc, as well as Prudence Island, and Patience Island to help pay for the trip and his family's expenses while gone."[10]

Williams was accompanied by Baptist minister John Clarke, and while they succeeded in securing a new charter that reunited the colony on paper, it did nothing to quell the turbulence within. Williams served as president of Providence Plantations once again, from 1654 to 1657, but it was three years of turmoil.

In 1662, after the revolution in England was over and the monarchy reestablished, John Clarke was again dispatched to London with a letter of introduction from Williams declaring him as agent for the colony. His correspondence with the Crown to obtain a new charter for the Rhode Island was promising, particularly the ministers' hopes for a "lively experiment that a most flourishing civill state may stand…and best be maintained…with a full libertie in religious concernments." Williams and Clarke sought to finally legally grant the inhabitants of Rhode Island and Providence Plantations freedom of conscience, or the right to practice whatever religion they chose without fear of persecution.

In the spring of 1662, Governor John Winthrop Jr. of Connecticut visited London as well and obtained a new charter for his colony. This charter called into question the boundaries between Connecticut and Rhode Island and Winthrop's stake in the so-called Atherton purchases, in which large tracts of land claimed by Rhode Island were sold to individuals loyal to Connecticut. This presented a more viable threat back home.

For as much as Clarke and Williams sought to expand the boundaries of religious freedom, the majority of their co-inhabitants sought land and an expansion of their own personal property and enterprise. Williams had sought, in the words of a modern transcriber, to "cool the land fever" that had gripped the colony. In December 1661, Williams affirmed the boundaries of the colony as determined by the original deed from Narragansett sachems and reiterated his intentions in founding Providence to be "a shelter for persons distressed of conscience." By 1662, however, landholders in the town sought to solidify their control over lands allotted to them as well as gain control of sizeable portions of land both east and west of the established borders.

Clarke had gone to England to negotiate on the colony's behalf and essentially wrote the new charter, which included the unprecedented liberty of conscience for the colony and also gave greater corporate powers; promised protection, at least on paper, to the indigenous people from attack from Massachusetts and Connecticut (largely so that treaties and land obtained by Rhode Islanders would be preserved); and established fishing rights offshore.

The new charter also gave the colony's assembly the authority to wade through the contentious cases of land disputes, though they would take many more years to resolve, and effectively allowed landholders to greatly expand their holdings, which would give rise to the great estates that became known as the Narragansett Plantations. Thus the pattern of British attempts at another plantation venture continued with the indigenous peoples of the location expelled or enslaved and the resulting lands fought over by large investors as the yeoman farmers who had settled there fought to save their own existence.

No matter how potent our mythologies have become, from Winthrop's vision of a "city on a hill," to the Pilgrims' community of faith and friendship and Roger Williams's refuge for "liberty of conscience," the primary aim of colonizing was to provide goods for other colonies contained within Great Britain's vast empire—especially those reliant on slave labor.

Williams's lands at Cocumscussoc, where he transacted business but could also retreat for the comfort of his "beloved privacy," would become the site of one of the first northern plantations, as we know the term today, in North America.

This then is the story of these plantations, their role in New England's commerce and slavery, and the common thread that inextricably tied the northern states to southern slavery leading up to and beyond the time of the Civil War.

HORSES, CATTLE AND SUNDRY GOODS TO THE WEST INDIES

These New England plantations, while small in comparison to those of the later southern antebellum period, operated on slave labor and supplied the "vital components" needed for the Caribbean plantations.

Historian Eric Kimball wrote that "New England ships, crewed by New England men, carried fish, livestock, timber, and slaves to the sugar colonies in the West Indies"[11] Those ships returned with sugar, molasses and rum, the ingredients that would soon make the trading of enslaved Africans the most lucrative commerce in the region.

In those early years, the fleet of ships bringing goods from New England would prove to be equally valuable to the islands. As the governor of Barbados acknowledged in 1667, "His Majesties colonies in these parts cannot in tyme of peace prosper, nor in tyme of war subsist, with a correspondence [in other words, trade] with the people of New England."[12]

Barbados, as with other American plantations, had begun in 1627 with the settlement of a handful of yeoman farmers who "sought to replicate the institutions of their homeland and to create a quality of life and an environment superior to that which they had left behind."

The vast archipelago that comprises the West Indies includes three sets of islands known as the Greater Antilles, made up of Cuba, Hispaniola, Jamaica and Puerto Rico, and the Lesser Antilles, which lies like a jeweled necklace on the channel between Puerto Rico and the coast of Venezuela, encompassing forty inhabitable islands, including Antigua and Barbados, among the many islets and rocks of the chain.[13] The Bahamas comprise

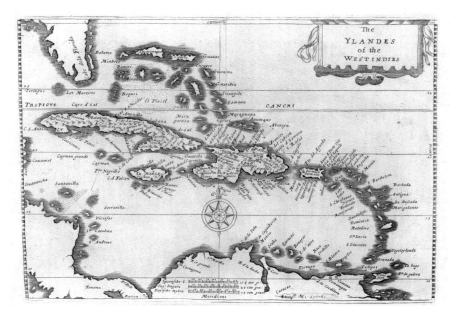

"The Ylands of the West Indies," Thomas Gage, London, 1655. *Courtesy of the John Carter Brown Library at Brown University.*

another thirty inhabitable islands north of Cuba, among an even larger outcrop of islets and rocks.

The Spanish were the first to colonize islands in the Indies, but through the course of the seventeenth century, the Dutch, French and English wrested control of the islands and their surrounding waters to establish trading posts and plantations. Though each colony vied for competition among the European vessels, when conflict arose, subsequent peace treaties of Breda, Ryswick and Utrecht meant that with a pair of exceptions, the map of the Caribbean remained unchanged from the 1660s to the 1760s.[14]

Historian Richard B. Sheridan summarized the change that came to the islands:

> In the course of several decades the West Indies experienced a marked decline in the number of yeoman farmers, small plantations, and white servants at the same time that there emerged numerous sugar plantations each of substantial acreage, capital, and slave labor force. Food crops and livestock tended to be sacrificed for cane—thus leading the sugar plantations to import many of their food, livestock, and wood from England, Ireland, and New England.[15]

An early modern history of trade in the island noted that the colonists of Barbados "needed to import increasingly large supplies of heavy timbers, lumber, barrel staves, and hoops; and for turning their mills, they needed more oxen and horses than Dutch ships could bring from Europe." Of cattle, historian Edmund S. Morgan observed, "Land in the West Indies was too valuable to be devoted to food products, and sugar plantations were eager to buy live cattle....They needed live cattle not only to turn the mills but also to dung their land as the canes exhausted it."[16]

In 1647, an epidemic illness spread from New England to the islands; some five or six thousand people perished on the islands of St. Christopher and Barbados. This was accompanied by an extensive drought that destroyed what produce and livestock the islands contained. This increased the demand for goods, cattle and horses from New England, which had been considered a poor and barren region of North America.

Such was the demand that Virginia joined New England in the export of cattle to the islands. Rhode Island sent a shipment of domesticated cattle to Barbados as early as 1649, but Virginia oxen were considered the best bred in the colonies. New England then, quickly became a prime provider of horses to the Caribbean.

Rev. William Hubbard, the early chronicler of New England history, noted that a vessel left Charlestown, Massachusetts, with eighty horses bound for Barbados in the summer of 1648.[17] The majority of horses, however, came predominantly from Rhode Island and Connecticut. Various species of equines had trod the colony's soil since the 1650s, when investors, including John Hull and William Brenton from Massachusetts Bay, partnered to purchase much of what was then called Point Judah Neck. The area known today as Point Judith is the southernmost tip of Galilee, whose "neck" juts out into Narragansett Bay just southwest of Newport. William Coddington of that city as well as Francis Brinley held stake in adjacent land to Brenton's on the neck, leading to a dispute concerning one herd of horses that was shipped out in 1656.

In southern Rhode Island, great swaths of land had been grabbed in what became known as the Pettasquamscutt Purchase, a deal long disputed by the indigenous tribe of the region. Among the five purchasers was Thomas Mumford (the others being John Porter, Samuel Wilbore, Samuel Wilson and the aforementioned Hull), whose purchase included much of the swamp where the Narragansett winter encampment lay.

By the 1660s, William Brenton had acquired 2,000 acres of Point Judith on which he kept cattle and bred both draft horses and the famed

Minister Ezra Stile's *Map of Southwestern Rhode Island*, showing Boston Neck. *Courtesy of the John Carter Brown Library at Brown University.*

Narragansett Pacers. Another 265 acres on Conanicut Island were likely the grazing lands for the 1,600 sheep he had accrued by the time of his death in 1674.

Goldsmith John Hull of Boston first envisioned the breeding of what became known as the Narragansett Pacer when he wrote to Benedict Arnold and other partners: "I have sometimes thought that if we the partners of Pointe Juda Necke did procure a very good breed of large and fair mares and stallions and that no mongrel breed might come among them…we might have a very choice breed…& in a few years might draw of considerable numbers & ship them for Barbados Nevis or such ports of the Indies."

Most of the horses shipped from pastures owned by the early planters were sent to Newport, then the port of choice for international trade, though Providence would not lag far behind. The horses were corralled on deck, despite the risk of some being swept overboard or crashing on the slippery deck during a storm.

These were, according to historian John Miller, not yet the famed pacers that would later catch the fancy of the planter elites, but mainly draft horses to turn the wheels of the sugar mills and others to be used as carriage horses. When Quaker John Fox visited Barbados in 1671, he was met by merchant John Rouse with the carriage and horses of Colonel Champlain, a native Rhode Islander. Rouse informed his visitor that the planters on the island regularly sent to Rhode Island and Connecticut for "matching carriage horses."

John Josseylyn commented in 1677 that in much of New England, horse breeders "let them roam all the year abroad and seldom provide any fodder for them." At home, ordinary nags were used more often than pacers, and they bore families to church, carried travelers from inn to inn and pulled light wagons of surplus cheese, eggs and vegetables to market but were seldom used for draft purposes.[18]

Other vessels journeyed to Rhode Island in search of horses. In December 1661, the *Black Horse*, a four-hundred-ton ship from

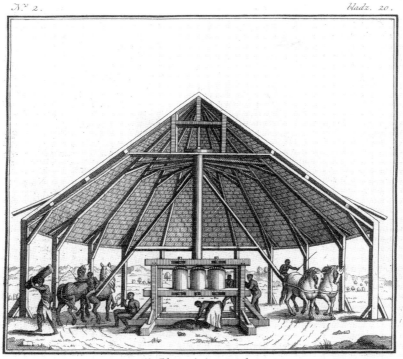

N.º 2.   bladz. 20.

V. v. d. Plaats junior, excud. 1770.

Sugar mill driven by horses, Philippe Fermin (1721–1813). Published by V.van der Plaats, 1770. *Courtesy of the John Carter Brown Library at Brown University.*

Amsterdam, sailed to Carlisle Bay with a crew of thirty-two men and a cargo of fifty-two horses. They found no additional cargo to bring back to Europe and so sailed to Rhode Island for additional horses to trade at Barbados. Once arrived at Narragansett Bay, the crew unloaded salt and sand and took on fresh water and hay, along with "thirty fine horses," salted meat, meal, bread and staves.[19]

After setting out on March 6, the ship lost a mast and returned to Newport for repairs. The ship set sail again after taking on additional water and hay and arrived safely in Bridgetown on April 30. It had lost half of the Dutch horses in the crossing but only one of those taken on in Rhode Island.[20]

Early vessels that plied the trade included the *Tryall*, a well-traveled ketch owned by merchants William Richardson and Nicholas Davis, which was sent on two voyages from Newport to Barbados in the year 1663–64, carrying sixteen horses each time.[21] By 1681, the governor of the colony acknowledged that horses were "the principille export" of Rhode Island and would remain as such for nearly a century.

Family Ties

Some New Englanders moved to Barbados to oversee the family interests. Others moved to the islands for a fresh start. One of the first was John Seabury of Boston, removing himself and his eldest son, John, to Barbados after 1642. Seabury's granddaughter Sarah, born in Duxbury, Massachusetts, would later marry Joseph Harbin, a well-to-do merchant of St. Michaels, who owned plantations in Jamaica and South Carolina.[22]

William Vassal was one of the original founders of the Massachusetts Bay Colony, but a man of Presbyterian rather than Puritan views, and he soon returned to England. He returned to the colony in 1635, settling in Roxbury, where according to Reverend Hubbard, he was "never at rest, but when he was in the fire of contention," being active with petitioners and a sometime pamphleteer. After a defeat in 1648, he left the colony, and "went to the Barbadoes, the torrid zone being more agreeable to those of his disposition."[23] Once there, he also found success in St. Michaels as a merchant and planter.[24]

Nathaniel Maverick, the son of Samuel Maverick, was born in the grand house his father built on Noddles Island in Boston Harbor. The elder Maverick was well known for his hospitality, opening the house to many visitors, including John Josselyn, who recorded the visit from July 1638. His son Nathaniel removed to Barbados shortly before 1656 and engaged as an agent for his father, who was soon importing sugar onto the island. Nathaniel's son John became the patriarch of what would become a well-established South Carolina plantation family.[25]

More young men and women married into families already located there. In 1675, James Borden, whose family was of Portsmouth, Rhode Island, moved to the tropical island. By 1680, he was married, with a plantation near Bridgetown that produced enough goods to establish himself as a merchant, kept an apprentice and owned fourteen slaves.

Borden "dealt chiefly with horses with Walter Newbury and other Quaker Friends in Rhode Island and Barbados."[26]

Borden was far from alone in his venture. A fair number of New Englanders transported themselves to the West Indies during this period of early commerce with the sole purpose of becoming partners with merchant friends in New England. As historian Carl Bridenbaugh noted, "Younger sons seeking their fortune were entering trade in the West Indies with the support of London relatives themselves anxious to profit from the importation of colonial goods. Often these families had kinsmen on the American mainland who joined in the growing enterprise." Bridenbaugh added that "many marriages… illustrated the gradual joining of mercantile and planting farmers of the West Indies with New England and the low countries, as well as with Britain, and which would in time fuse them into a sort of Atlantic Society."

Among the most notable of these was John Winthrop's son Samuel,   who married into a Dutch mercantile family on Barbados and eventually took his bride and trading interests to Antigua. In September 1658, early on during the course of his education in trade, Winthrop Sr. wrote to his son a somewhat worrisome letter: "I have not received any intelligence by any letters or other ways from you but a sad report which is spread abroad in all the plantations.…[Y]ou should write every way that offers, either by Barbados, Virginia, or other opportunity."

Slaves in Barbados, published for Sir Richard Phillips & Co., Bridge St., London, 1820. *Courtesy of the John Carter Brown Library at Brown University.*

William Brenton had been dealing with Barbados for some years when he sent his twenty-two-year-old future son-in-law Peleg Sanford to Barbados "to learn all he could about the trading opportunities opened up by the 'sugar revolution'."[27] In addition to the horse breeding grounds on Point Judith, Brenton's Rocky Farm in Newport included much of the land that borders the present Hammersmith Farm and holdings along Ocean Drive and Fort Adams, amounting to several thousand acres on which he reputedly held, at one time, a flock of 1,100 sheep.[28]

On his return, Peleg Sanford shipped many of the horses bred from this partnership, as well as mares and geldings from the Hutchinson farm, from Newport between 1662 and 1668. He essentially served as the middleman for those Bostonians who had invested in Rhode Island lands, which barely needed "improving" into lush pastures and breeding grounds. He held a monopoly on the cattle, horses and provisions from these farms and shipped them exclusively to his brothers, William and Elisha, merchants in Barbados who resold them at exaggerated prices.

When widower Thomas Newton married Joan Smith in Dutch territory without permission of her father or authorities, the couple fled to Barbados, where he became the connection to commerce on the island for brother-in-law Richard Smith Jr. at Cocumscussoc. When the plantation there was at its height under Daniel Updike, it was his stepson Joseph Wanton who was the connection in Surinam. The young Wanton was named in a letter from James Bowditch as one of those "whose small purses will not admit of cheap molasses of which Jos. Wanton of Rhoad Island is one who has risen the price of molasses from seven and a half to thirteen, the planters say the price is too great and would willingly fix it at eight stivers."

Other merchants had their origins in families already fixed in the West Indies whose descendants came to Rhode Island. Such was the case of Abraham Redwood the elder, born in Bristol, England, who later facilitated trading ventures between London and Jamaica. He settled in Antigua in 1687.

Richard Dunn wrote of the land, "Compared to its mountainous neighbors, Antigua is nearly flat, with a broad, central plain rimmed by low limestone hills on the windward side, and high volcanic hills on the leeward side....[T]he early planters cleared the Acacia and logwood forests that covered the interior of the island and converted it to cane fields. Since the entire island is swept entirely by breezez, they erected windmills on every sun baked hillside."[29] At the time of his arrival, barely half the arable

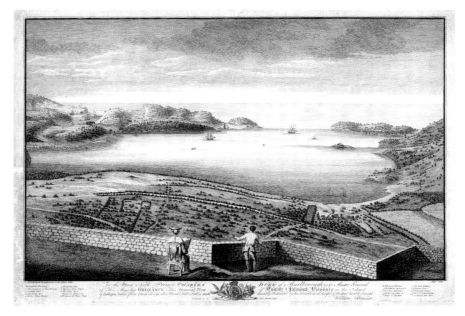

View of English and Falmouth Harbours in the Island of Antigua, engraving by William Brasier, 1757. *Courtesy of the John Carter Brown Library at Brown University.*

land on the island was claimed for improvement, and Antigua was known to be an island of "moderate, rather small plantations; producing very little besides sugar and rum."[30]

Nonetheless, when Redwood married Mehetable Langford, daughter of Jonas Langford, a prominent landowner, he obtained by marriage a sizeable sugar plantation named Cassada Gardens that held a large slave population. Redwood moved to Newport sometime after 1715. He died there in 1729 at the age of sixty-four. His son Abraham Redwood Jr. (1709–1788) stood to inherit the property, as the eldest son, Jonas Langford Redwood, died by a fall from a horse in 1724.[31]

Long distance family members urged Abraham Redwood the younger to return home and settle his affairs—in fact, settle in, if he so desired. A letter from Richard Nugent in January 1731 informed Redwood of the death of his grandmother in Barbados and the pressing need for him to determine an overseer of his property in Antigua. Nugent offered his own services "as you always have been my friend, I am in hopes you will continue….[Y]ou may depend I shall study to merritt your favours, consider I shall not keep any of your Negroes out of your field. I have House Negroes enough of my own, and that advantage will only be considerable in your way as you want a great many more than you have to settle your Estate."[32]

But Redwood resisted. Even as these endearments from his family were sent, he was reluctant to leave what must have been a comfortable living as the agent for the plantation in Newport, selling the sugar to agents for London and local merchants as well. He corresponded frequently but did not travel to Cassada Gardens until 1737 and then stayed three years, improving the already flourishing plantation. During his time there, his sloop *Humbird* brought twenty cattle, nine horses and forty-one hogs as well as 120 pounds of cheese and 1,300 pounds of hay from Newport to his estate.

He returned to Rhode Island a wealthy man, purchased 143 acres of land in Portsmouth and built an estate that let him live a lordly, or planter-like, lifestyle. A visitor recorded, "We saw Mr. Redwood's garden…one of the finest I…ever saw in my life.…[I]t groes all sorts of West Indian fruits…it also has west Indian flowers…"

Slaves from both Redwood's estate in Antigua and his farm in Portsmouth seem to have been exchanged at times, much in the way that planters and merchants sent troublesome indigenous slaves or enslaved individuals no longer needed to the West Indies. "I send you two Negroes," wrote Nugent in a letter sent in April 1731. "If you like them keep them and give my Account credit for what you think they are worth. the Negroe man is a piece of a Saylor and a fine Papa Slave—cost thirty pounds Sterling out of the Ship. the Negroe woman is a fine Slave. I had another which is a better…but suspected something I intended against her, on which shee's given us the Slip this morning, but I hope to have her againe before Pope sailes."[33]

Abraham's half brother William Redwood (1726–1815) and his nephew Jonas worked in partnership with William Vernon in the slave trading ventures of the *Titt Bitt* in 1756 and the *Venus* in 1758, as well as the voyages of the ship *Cassada Garden*, named for the

The elegant "garden house," a remnant from the Malbone garden in Newport. From *Gardens of Colony and State: Gardeners and Gardens of the American Republic before 1840. Author's collection.*

family plantation.[34] In Newport, William Redwood worked as a merchant in partnership with Elias Bland. He moved to Philadelphia in 1772 and conducted business there. In 1782, after Jonas's death, he removed to Antigua and helped maintain the plantation until his return to Philadelphia in 1787 and resumed business in that city.

As Pares noted in his history *Yankees and Creoles*, "Some personal links between the northern and the sugar colonies survived until the Revolution: the Redwood's of Newport, the Livingston's of New York, and the Dickinson's of Philadelphia, continued to hold West Indian property, and the descendants of other West Indian families…lived in the northern colonies."[35]

Growth of the American Plantations

To fully understand the growth of these enterprises, we must start around 1649, when Roger Williams, the founder of Rhode Island, and Richard Smith of New Amsterdam and later of Taunton, both had trading rights in and around the lands and waters of Cocumscussoc. In 1651, Williams, needing to raise money for a voyage to England, sold his rights and property to Richard Smith, including a freshwater spring and the "little island for goates which the old Sachem, deceased, Lent me for that use."

For many years, Smith hired overseers to live at his property on Cocumscussoc, but around 1650, he was there permanently and began to expand the trading post into a working farm. A decade later, with his son and daughter-in-law Hester Smith in the household, the family used his wife Joan's recipe to produce cheese. This export would prove to reach great popularity among merchants in the coastal trade of the time. Smith's sloop *Welcome* regularly sailed this route, transporting the family between New York, Taunton and Rhode Island.

Smith and his son Richard Jr. "succeeded in monopolizing most of the trade of the country and 'Mr. Smith's' was for years the principal meeting place in Narragansett."[36] Historian Bernard Bailyn believed that among the rising merchant families, "The Smiths made the most of the brief flourishing of the Narragansett fur trade and, alone among the merchant families of Rhode Island, founded their dealings with cattle and agricultural produce on this early form of enterprise."[37]

Father and son would also purchase extensive tracts of land in 1659, as part of the disputed "Atherton purchases," which they were allowed to keep

A view of "Queen's Island" at Cocumscussoc. *Photo by the author.*

and "improve" in the coming years. Upon Smith Sr.'s death in 1666, his son Richard inherited the property. Roger Williams testified of Smith Jr. that "since [Richard Smith Sr.'s] departure, his…son, Capt. Richard Smith, hath kept possess (with much acceptation, both with English and Pagans) of his Father's howsing, lands, and meadoes, with great emprovement."[38] In September 1671, Smith Jr. wrote Connecticut governor John Winthrop Jr., "My ocacions hath been much to fitt outt our ship for Barbados, which nowe is redy within 3 or 4 days."

The success of these endeavors brought some dangers from pirates and privateers, along with economic gains. Richard Smith Jr. wrote to John Winthrop Jr. from Wickford, Rhode Island, in May 1673, "Here arrived a kaitch 4 days since att Newport from Barbados; she was chased 48 ours by a ship about 100 leges from hence. Its judged some sculking men of ware may anoye this cost."[39] In August of that same year he reported, "I had leters from the Master of my vessel, dated June 12th Newfoundland and who informes me that only one shipe from England ther this yeare. A Plymouth man who was taken 3 times by the Duch [illegible] reports that our Nacion lost 1000 sayle of ships last yeare. Great prepacions by the 3 contesting Nacions."

By 1675, however, the rebellion by indigenous peoples over lands and cultural impositions had destabilized the economy the colonial authorities established. Smith invited troops from neighboring Connecticut and Massachusetts to encamp on his property and use it as a base for raids against Narragansett encampments though they had pledged neutrality in the war. The move brought the war to Rhode Island, and by the following spring, the trading post at Cocumscussoc had burned to the ground and nearly every house between Warwick and Providence had been razed.

Within two years of the end of King Philip's War, Richard Smith Jr. received compensation from Connecticut and Massachusetts, allowing him to rebuild at Cocumscussoc. The house Smith Jr. built was a large, slant-roofed dwelling with dormers in front and an extended front entryway. Two square front rooms faced the cove, with a long, low room in the rear of the house for dairy and cheese production. No longer a trading post, the house and property now assumed the role and look of a plantation. Smith gradually increased his cattle holdings and production of cheese to include the long-standing product in shipments to Barbados, including the plantation in Christ Church owned by the family of his brother-in-law Thomas Newton.

On his death in 1692, Richard Smith Jr.'s property included the Great House, a two-story warehouse in which raw materials such as caulk and lumber were stored, a shop and a two-story stone house that included a kitchen. Smith's inventory included 135 head of cattle, 30 sheep, 20 swine and 3 horses. He enslaved eight people: two grown men, five African boys and an elderly woman. While trade still played an important role at Cocumscussoc, the increase of livestock suggests that Smith had invested heavily in the plantation economy.

The property of Cocumscussoc was inherited by Richard Smith's nephew Lodowick Updike, or Opdyke, as the family name was in Manhattan. The young Updike had lived at the trading house since 1660, when he was fourteen years old, and was certainly familiar with the farm's production and exports. At the time of his inheritance, he was newly married to Abigail Newton, a marriage that in and of itself created important connections between the two wealthy families. That wealth would be visited upon their son Daniel, born in 1693, who would live his entire life in privilege and luxury. His descendant Wilkins Updike wrote, "His education was carefully carried on by tutors at home....The young Daniel it is asserted, was a great student and had a reputation as a penman. He was induced by a merchant of Barbados [perhaps John Chace, later his brother-in-law][40] to accompany him thither, tarrying there for some time and thus enlarging his information."[41]

The Chace family owned two adjoining plantations near Bridgetown, as shown on *A New Map of the Island of Barbados* (1676).[42] The young Updike was "admitted to the first circles of society on the island," visiting the parlors of the plantation owners' houses among this circle of wealthy landowners and slaveholders. He would have keenly observed "how the planters organized the plantations and how they best employed their slave labor."[43]

These lessons were applied on a smaller scale at Cocumscussoc. When Daniel Updike inherited the property, he was living in Newport and viewed Cocumscussoc as a summer residence. In 1730, he hired an overseer named Isaac Phillips and gave explicit instructions about the crops to be planted. Updike instructed Phillips to "plant 30 acres of maize, 30 acres of English corn, clear 10 acres of ground for meadow, and care for the orchards." Phillips was also given the right to cultivate his own quarter-acre kitchen garden.[44]

The probate inventory taken after Updike's death in 1757 suggests, as Cocumscussoc historian Neil Dunay observed, that he "shifted the farm away from the Smith model of cattle for cheese production to sheep for wool and more particularly for meat (mutton) which was packed in butts (hence the need for cooper tools listed in the backroom) and shipped to Caribbean plantations."[45] Updike undertook this shift in production while

"Smith's Castle," the elegant house of the Updike plantation in the colonial era. *Photo by the author.*

the other Narraganset plantations were still making great quantities of cheese based on the Smith recipe.

The plantation at Cocumscussoc reached its peak about the mid-eighteenth century, encompassing some three thousand acres and exporting goods from both the stone dock at Cocumscussoc and Richard Updike's dock in Wickford, which included a warehouse and a large wharf that jutted out toward Cornelius Island. Daniel Updike left nineteen enslaved people on the plantation in the charge of his heir Lodowick Updike, who raised a large family at Cocumscussoc and oversaw the transformation of the plantation during the Revolutionary War and its aftermath. The loss of slaves, both those who had fought for their freedom and those later emancipated in 1784, as well as the loss of trade, was a death knell to the planter economy. The Updikes' attempted to diversify at the turn of the nineteenth century by expanding the family trade into Asia, before financial misfortune, the embargo of 1807–9 and the War of 1812, forced the last heir, Wilkins Updike, to sell the plantation on December 31 of that year.

By the mid-eighteenth century, New England plantations had increased trade "with the assistance of masses of African slaves…[and] turned to raising staple articles of produce for the European market and importing luxuries for the planter elite and foodstuffs, clothing, plantation tools, and equipment for the white indentured servants and the black slaves."[46] Cocumscussoc was the earliest and northernmost plantation of the wealthy landowners in South County, who became known as the "Narragansett Planters." As Rhode Island historian Christian McBurney noted in his study of these men:

> *Though their reign was short-lived, the Narragansett Planters succeeded to a significant extent in developing a plantation based economy. On a wider scale, they were New England counterparts to other colonials who intentionally created rural gentry communities.…Wealth derived from commercial farming enabled the planters of the Narragansett Country and elsewhere to attain their highest aspiration: to imitate the lifestyle of the English country gentry, who enjoyed social prominence, political influence, and a life of leisure and privilege.*[47]

These Narragansett plantations would all contribute to their sister plantations of the Caribbean.

Rowland Robinson, an inhabitant of Newport in 1675, took advantage of the "vacant lands" the colony made available after King Philip's War, buying 300 acres "east by the salt water, west by Petticomcit pond" on

View of Rowland Robinson House, Old Boston Neck Road, Saunderstown, Rhode Island. *Photo by the author.*

Boston Neck, where he built a farmhouse, and then another 3,000 acres, a tract so vast that it stretched to the border of Connecticut. He then sold the acreage in parcels of 100 to 150 acres, using the money from these land speculations to invest in his expansive farming enterprise.[48] Robinson also kept a large dairy, his preference being "blanket cows," and he was said to have kept a herd of "one hundred blanket cows…neither more, no less."[49]

Robinson, like other planters, bred Narragansett Pacers, a horse that in the forty years of trading with Barbados had proven to be a favorite riding horse among the planter elite, just as they were in Narragansett. In 1705, his inventory lists 64 horses. By the time of his death, he was the largest stockholder in the region, holding some 175 head of cattle, a large flock of 666 sheep and 51 horses. His will gave his son nine slaves and 680 acres of land.[50]

Robinson's son William continued to expand the family holdings and the breeding of the Narragansett Pacer. One account attributes the improvement of the breed to the introduction of an Andalusian stallion imported by William Robinson. A contemporary of Daniel Updike, Robinson, too, lived the planter lifestyle with a mind to civic affairs, serving as the deputy from South Kingstown for nearly a decade before being elected deputy governor in 1745 and again in 1747. He married twice and raised thirteen children on his large estate at Silver Lake, which at the time of his death in 1751 was valued at over £21,000. An inventory of his estate included 105 milk cows, as well as heifers, 17 oxen and 2 tons of cheese.

Grandson Rowland Robinson Jr. also expanded the family enterprise. By the 1760s, he was exporting prodigious amounts of cheese, milk, oats, hay, sheep and horses. This generation of Robinsons also invested in the slave trade. *The Economic Activities of the Narragansett Planters*, a locally famous mural created during the WPA years on the wall of the South Kingstown Post Office and now in the South County History Center, is said to depict the loading of Robinson's boats at the dock near his farm.

His neighbor Robert Hazard, the grandson and namesake of one of the founders of South Kingstown, was said to have shipped one hundred horses per year at the height of his trade. The younger Hazard had inherited a large parcel of land near Worden's Pond on the death of his father and expanded his holdings and breeding grounds on the southern end of Boston Neck. Hazard dealt in all manner of draft horses. In 1750, he purchased a three-year-old horse for £150. A year later, he paid £55 for a thirteen-year-old "bay mare with a white nose." As planters shipped more horses, prices for the few remaining seems to have dramatically increased. By 1765, Hazard was paying out £244 for "an old black trotting mare." I.P. Hazard, the grandson of Robert Hazard, wrote of the height of the breeding of the pacer that "my grandfather…raised about one hundred annually, and often loaded two vessels a year with them, and other products of his farm, which sailed directly from the South Ferry to the West Indies."[51]

Thomas Hazard held ownership in the sloop *Dolphin* at Newport in 1761, which is listed in Coughtry's *The Notorious Triangle*. Both planters shipped and received goods, horses and slaves from the docks at the South Ferry on Boston Neck.[52] Other planters of this era relied on the ferries themselves and brought their goods to be loaded and delivered to Aaron Lopez in Newport, who held interest in more than thirty vessels sailing from that port. By 1748, the docks at the South Ferry had become overrun; the few boats that left were "crowded with men, women, and children" as well as "horses, hogs, sheep, and cattle to the intolerable inconvenience, annoyance and delay of men and business." Neighboring planter John Gardiner thus urged the colony's assembly to expand the port at the South Ferry landing.

Many of the Narragansett planters supplied the firm of Lopez and Rivera with goods for market. Aaron Lopez's account book lists numerous purchases of hemp, tobacco, apples, potatoes, peas and beans as well as livestock. In 1767, Lopez purchased 2,003 pounds of beef for export from planter Hezekiah Babcock. He also purchased 1, 438 pounds from Nathaniel

View of the present site of the South Ferry, now home to the University of Rhode Island Bay Campus. *Photo by the author.*

Gardiner that same year. In 1769, he purchased 100 sheep from Rowland Robinson and another 60 from George Irish for export. But as Robert K. Fitts pointed out, "The Planter's most important crop was hay which was sold to Caribbean and Southern planters to feed their livestock."[53]

Farther south in Charlestown, Rhode Island, the Stanton family built its own small empire between bordering colonies beginning with land given to Thomas Stanton in 1655. There he built the beginnings of a great house, the third-oldest structure in Rhode Island. Stanton originally founded a trading business with William Whiting at Hartford, Connecticut, where the pair created a monopoly on the fur trade. After Whiting's death in 1647, "Stanton moved to the border region between Rhode Island and Connecticut where, in 1650, he was granted control of the fur trade along the Pawcatuck River."[54]

Stanton's son Daniel moved to Barbados to act as the "overseas partner" with the family firm. Thomas Stanton & Sons shipped corn, beans, dried fish, jerked venison, salt and flour to Barbados aboard two vessels, the *Alexander* and *Martha*, built by Daniel in 1681, and an older vessel built by his brother Thomas Stanton Jr. The sloops returned to Pawcatuck laden with sugar, molasses and rum, as well as the occasional slave, according to one Connecticut historian, "only 3–4 each year."[55] As with other New England colonies, these West Indian slaves would have been integrated with the indigenous and African slaves already bound on southern New England plantations.

Thomas Stanton died in 1677. His son Daniel died sometime before 1688 in Barbados, leaving a wife and child. Thomas Stanton's nephew Joseph Stanton inherited the Rhode Island farm and expanded the house, building the last addition around 1740, by which time the farm had become a large dairy concern.

Joseph Stanton Sr. built a house of his own in 1739 on a low bluff overlooking the family's horse breeding grounds, which stretched beyond to Quonochontaug pond and the shoreline of Block Island Sound. His son Joseph Stanton Jr. was born in the family home on July 19, 1739. The son continued the family tradition of entering the military, being commissioned as a second lieutenant in the Rhode Island regiment raised for the expedition against Canada during the French and Indian War in 1759.

Stanton Jr. went on to a political career and served in the General Assembly from 1748 to 1755. His estate and wealth grew considerably; an old account attests that "he owned a lordship in Charlestown[,] a tract of four miles long and two miles wide, kept 40 horses, as many slaves, and made a great dairy."

Some planters in the West Indies and Virginia horse breeders wanted pacers with such urgency than rather than wait for exports to arrive, they

The Stanton Homestead, Charlestown, Rhode Island. *Photo by the author.*

maintained local buyers in Narragansett to snap up the best animals.[56] I.P. Hazard considered the great demand for the pacers to be "one of the causes of the loss of that famous horse here," especially with the development of sugar plantations in Cuba, where the demand for the horse grew as well. Hazard wrote, "The Planters suddenly became rich and wanted the Pacers for themselves, and their wives and daughters to ride."

An agent from the island, sent exclusively to buy horses, "made his home at the Rowland Brown house on Tower Hill where he commenced purchasing and shipping until all the good ones were sent off."[57] These horses had become so prized that they were placed in slings upon the deck—unlike less valued horses corralled on a slippery deck, they would keep safe in the dangerous swells that swept many horses overboard.[58]

Sometime after 1720, the Ten Rod Road between Voluntown, Connecticut, and Wickford, Rhode Island, was completed. Its name derived from the agreed-on measurement of 165 feet being suitable for driving cattle, and the road increased the trade the seaport had developed early with the West Indies. Wickford was largely owned and laid out by the Updike family of the Cocumscussoc Plantation. The traffic on the road—cattle, sheep and wagons carrying staves and ship timber from the farms and forests of eastern Connecticut—would continue unabated until the Revolutionary War, when the British blockade closed the port of Wickford.

Trade from Providence

The shipping of horses from Providence would begin in earnest with the ventures of James Brown, a marine captain who set up a merchandise house along the Providence River. Biographer James Hedges wrote, "While keeping store in Providence with one hand, Captain Brown was expanding his Caribbean trade with the other. His ships made many voyages to the British Islands, to those not in the British domain, and to Surinam, or Dutch Guinea."[59]

Brown often advertised for "Horses Suitable for Surinam" in the *Providence Gazette* and relied on a man named Davis from Pomfret, Connecticut, to procure horses and other goods for him: "[P]lease to gett tan horsis for me that is sutabil to go to Surray nam [Surinam] and bring tham downe naxte Munday Cum fortnit and bring me all the Butter and ottes that falls your way."[60]

Detail of the Providence, Rhode Island waterline from John Updike's Merchant Certificate, 1791. *Courtesy of the Cocumscussoc Archives.*

Where Davis secured the horses for Brown is unknown, though evidence about how far-reaching goods from the West Indies had become, and how difficult it would have been to transfer horses from the area, is found in an early description of "Kennedy," later called Hampton, Connecticut:

> *The road known as Windham Road had been opened and brought much traffic to the settlement on route to Old Windham and Norwich. A store had been opened by Benjamin Bidlock where home-spun and farm produce could be exchanged for West India goods which were brought into the region either with ox-sleds or in barrels swung between two poles behind a horse.*[61]

The old trails leading to and from the settlement had been "widened into unbridged 'tote' roads so rough and impassable that it took a whole day to travel a few miles."[62] It is possible that Davis made his way to the Nipmuc path and then to New London and a ship bound for Rhode Island, but it is more likely, if he traveled overland, that he took the road west from Pomfret laid out in 1731, a highway that "afforded direct travel to the Boston Post Road, over Pomfret Hill" and would have gone directly through South County on the way to Providence. If this was Davis's route, he likely procured horses in Narragansett.

Brown exchanged the horses for sugar and molasses in Surinam. Such was the traffic to and from the West Indies that the Molasses Act was enacted in 1733, charging Brown and other importers a tax of six pence per gallon. Brown, like other merchants, often circumvented the tax by having their ships divert from ports where custom officials were stationed, unloading certain goods in hidden coves or on one of the many small islands that dotted the coast.

For sixteen years, Captain James Brown expanded his enterprise, growing from his workhorses the *Four Bachelors* and *Truth and Delight*, to holding whole or part interest in the sloops *Dolphin, Rainbow, Hopewell, Humbird* and *Mary*, the first slave-trading vessel to sail from Providence.[63]

On Captain Brown's death in 1739, his younger brother Obadiah took over his affairs in Providence. Within a decade, Obadiah Brown had expanded the family business to include part ownership in the schooner *Ranger*, an unnamed privateer sloop, the brigantine *Warren* and the sloops *Sarah* and *Bachelor*, which made regular runs to the Caribbean. By the 1750s, his ships were unloading and taking on cargo in the ports of Cuba and the Bay of Honduras.

Advertisement for horses from the *Providence Gazette. Courtesy of the author.*

The family shipping empire was inherited and improved by nephews John, James and Moses Brown. They helmed a firm that would dominate shipping from Providence through the eighteenth century.

A Bounty of Trade

Merchants like the Browns shipped a wide variety of goods to protect their cargo from a glut of one product or another when they reached their destination, a not uncommon occurrence, given competition in the islands from Dutch, French, Spanish and merchant vessels from London all arriving at the same ports of call.

As historian Richard Pares pointed out, the variety of goods shipped from Rhode Island and other southern New England colonies diversified early on. In 1661, a Dutch vessel arriving at the colony was loaded with "lumber for cask, salt meat, flour, bread, and 30 fine horses, for whom hay was shipped, twisted up into rope so as to say space."[64]

One of the Browns' first products was tobacco; they shipped a large quantity to Martinique as early as 1727, though the quality of the product appears to have been questionable. Rhode Island tobacco was said to be of a darker color than other types, perhaps from being packed in molasses barrels and often shipped to those locales from where the molasses had come.[65] A load of eight hogsheads was shipped to St. Eustatius in 1734, but in 1764, a similar lot was rejected in France as unsuitable.

The Browns and other merchants relied on the supply from their own manufacturing, goods from nearby farming communities and "the fishermen of Nantucket, from any other passerby or coastal speculator in goods fit for the West Indian market."[66]

The sloop *Mary Ann*, one of the Browns' vessels, left Providence in October 1766 bound for Surinam, and its manifest offers insight into a typical cargo:

> *100 Hogshead tobacco*
> *122 boxes spermaceti candles*
> *1,975 staves*
> *433 hoops*
> *4,000 bricks*
> *1,700 ft. heading*
> *8 horses with awning (and hay, oats, and water)*
> *3,000 bunches of onions*
> *35 hand-axes, 62 shaken hogsheads*
> *9 2/3 barrels beef, 5 2/3 barrels pork, 7 cwt. ship bread,*
> *3 firkins butter*
> *30 oars*
> *25 barrels tar*
> *12 barrels flour*
> *8 barrels oil*
> *3 shotes* [pigs]
> *and 50 kegs of oysters.*[67]

The Brown brothers exerted much effort to corner the market on tobacco shipped to Surinam. Though this scheme failed, their production and distribution of spermaceti candles held the market on their quality alone.[68]

It was ideal if the merchants from southern New England could sell their outgoing cargo for a price that would fill their holds for the return journey. Owners urged their captains to obtain other desired products at the West Indian ports. Some obtained cash or partial cargo for their goods and then proceeded on a "salt voyage," another commodity that could be had at "Salt Tortuga" and Bonaire, off the coast of Venezuela, as well as the Turk Islands, halfway between Hispaniola and the Bahamas.

Trade sometimes took a ship on a circuitous route back and forth across the Atlantic for a captain to gain the most profit. In December 1769, one

Edward Thorn, an overseer of a large plantation on St. Christopher, sailed to Rhode Island and purchased thirteen horses and mares. He returned successfully, losing only one horse, and sold the remainder at a great profit.

Such profit could still be made, as all of the West Indies, save for the Winward Islands, which had developed self-sufficiency, depended as heavily on the goods of New England as they had one hundred years before. According to historian Selwyn H.H. Carrington, "The dependency of the sugar colonies on the United States is nowhere more clearly illustrated than in the statistics giving the trade in provisions and lumber between each island and the United States between 1792–1806."

Carrington's research shows that the price of lumber especially rose to unprecedented heights after the Prohibitory Act in 1776 and never fell back to prewar levels. In Barbados, that amounted to a 440 percent increase. On some islands, the price of lumber was as much as 1220 percent above the prewar cost.

In addition, the prices of plantation supplies and foodstuffs for slaves also rose exorbitantly. The price per bushel of corn doubled in the years 1790–93, and barrels of herring, a chief source of protein, rose from forty-five to sixty-five shillings during the same period.

Little surprise then that commerce with the islands was still a growing enterprise for many in southern New England.

Connecticut's largest merchant farms, those over five hundred acres, included an inventory of cattle. Herds could number from the teens to over fifty head, and five of the largest landowners held flocks of over one hundred sheep. These farmers also engaged in producing large crops of wheat and flax, as well as large quantities of cider.[69]

The Connecticut River Valley also included large tobacco farms; the plant was introduced to the valley as early as 1640. By the eighteenth century, hogsheads of tobacco were being shipped to the West Indies, Europe and South America. As with other Southern New England plantations, these farms were run on the enslaved labor of indigenous people and Africans brought into the valley.

Another inter-colony connection was established with the acquisition of a large tract of land in Salem, Connecticut, by William Browne. At the suggestion of his father-in-law, Joseph Wanton, he hired John Mumford from the large slave-owning Rhode Island family to improve the land and oversee the plantation. Mumford arrived in Salem in 1759 and "entered immediately upon his labor employing a numerous gang of blacks."[70] The thirteen-thousand-acre plantation required sixty enslaved laborers to keep production high at its peak. By the time of the Revolutionary War, when

Tobacco barns
still remain in the
Connecticut River Valley,
as these in Gramby,
Connecticut. *Photo by
Rachel Holly Woods.*

the property was confiscated from its Tory owner, the nine remaining slaves on the property were sold for the benefit of the town coffers.

These plantations, among others in neighboring towns, made the port city of Middletown one of the busiest between Cape Cod and New York for trade with the West Indies.

Smaller merchants in Rhode Island who owned vessels in the minor ports of East Greenwich, Narragansett, Pawcatuck, Portsmouth, Warwick and Wickford entered into the Caribbean trade by the fishing industry. Historian Peter J. Coleman noted that by the early nineteenth century, "Wickford…for example, employed about six vessels in the Labrador Fishery. They sold some of the catch, either dried or salted, directly to vessels sailing for the Mediterranean….More often, they exchanged the catch in the West Indies for cargoes of molasses for the Narragansett Bay distilleries."[71]

Some South County planters directly dealt with like planters and ship owners in the southern colonies, as did Rowland Hazard, whose South County farm supplied merchants in South Carolina for their trade with the Caribbean between 1789 and 1807. Other owners of vessels "were not averse from having part of their efforts invested in Negroe slaves, who were to be had in the West Indies, whether Creole, or new Africans."

2

THE ENSLAVED ON LAND AND SEA

Slaves, Sugar and the Bounty of War

As demand for sugar in Great Britain increased, so did the desire for goods from New England colonies. As this demand increased, however, so did the market for goods from Great Britain. As Eric Kimball noted, "Trade with the West Indies provided the means for New Englanders to make payments on their debts to English creditors for their growing and seemingly insatiable appetite for European and English imports."[72]

Kimball wrote in his essay that the sale of goods was never quite enough to cover the debts New Englanders accrued for the items they favored. Other exports needed to be procured to cover the continuing losses, and the merchants of southern New England found one with the transport of another of those "vital components" needed on the sugar plantations of the Caribbean: slaves of both indigenous and African origin.

The first noted transport of indigenous people from the Dutch colony of Guiana to Barbados occurred in 1627, when Captain Henry Powell transported thirty-two Arawaks who had promised to teach the white settlers on the island "how to grow cotton, tobacco, and indigo and to facilitate trade between Barbados and the mainland colonies, all under the promise of living 'as free people'."[73] However, historian Linford Fisher noted, "Such freedom was short-lived, for some time after Powell's departure, other Barbadian planters took the Indians 'by force and made them slaves'."

An opportunity for British North American colonies to profit from the traffic in indigenous slaves came in the aftermath of the Pequot War in 1637. Rhode Island was also complicit in the distribution of slaves with vessels from Newport transporting many of those captured to the West

Indies. John Winthrop and Roger Williams both benefited from the taking of captives. Williams specifically requested a boy he had noticed during transport from Providence to Boston. The boy captive was the son of a Pequot chief who had died in the last battle of the war. Winthrop also kept and raised a boy as his servant.

Rhode Island was also complicit in the distribution of slaves, with vessels from Newport transporting many of those captured to the West Indies. That same year, participation in the African slave trade also began with ships from ports in southern New England.

Little is written in the early histories of these indigenous captives from New England, as Richard Ligon acknowledged in his colonial tract luring British traders to Barbados: "As for Indians, we have but few, and those fetcht from other Countries; some from neighboring Islands, some from the Maine [South America] which we make slaves."

But as historian Linford Fisher discovered in research for his project on indigenous slavery, "there seems to be a strange silence" in the halls of the imperial buildings that now house the records and inventories of the sugar plantations. He did find however, numerous mentions of indigenous slaves in wills, newspapers, court recordings and individual accounts.[74]

In one such document from 1652, a German-born indentured servant recorded that on the Barbadian plantation on which he worked, there were "one hundred Christians, one hundred negroes, and one hundred Indians in slavery."[75]

Massachusetts vessels began engaging in the slave trade as early as 1644, when three mariners—Miles Casson, Robert Shopton and James Smith—agreed to sail their vessels to Cape Verde and then to the west coast of Africa, agreeing that "whatsoever negars, or goods, gold, or silver, or other quality or vallew shallbe equally divided tunn for tunn, and man for man, in each severall ship."[76] The following April, Winthrop noted the return of one of these ships, recording in his journal that the ship had arrived with "wine and Sugar and salt, and some tobacco, which she had at Barbados in exchange for Africans."[77]

There is ample evidence to suggest that Massachusetts and Connecticut authorities were engaged in an effort to rid the regions of indigenous people at great profit. Winthrop's brother-in-law Emmanuel Downing wrote in the aftermath of the Pequot War that with another "just Warre…the lord should deliver [the Indians] into our hands, [and] wee might easily have men woemen and Children enough to exchange for Moores, which wilbe more gaynefull pilladge for us then wee conceive."[78]

KING PHILIP.

Published by S.G.Drake, Boston.

A nineteenth-century depiction of Metacom, or "King Philip." *Courtesy of the John Carter Brown at Brown University.*

The native uprising in North America that came to be known as King Philip's War would provide another opportunity for captives to be converted to cash or credit on Barbados and other islands. The opportunity came before the actual war began, when, as tensions rose, Massachusetts authorities invited the women, children and elderly of the regional tribes that could come under fire in the coming conflict to gather under their protection in Plymouth. Surprising numbers of trusting indigenous people arrived; they were then placed on ships and carted to the West Indies.

Rhode Island's Quaker government ostensibly kept the colony neutral, but Governor William Coddington's acceptance of Richard Smith Jr.'s request to assist troops in coming into Narragansett country nullified any prior efforts to keep the colony at peace. Massachusetts soldiers were especially brutal, raiding the fort of the elderly Queen Magnus as well as other sites nearby. As historian Douglas Leach wrote, "Before long the army had a sizeable collection of enemy prisoners, who were subsequently sold to Captain Davenport and transported to Aquidneck Island for safekeeping."

The brash Davenport would be among the first to fall at the battle of the Great Swamp days later, the captain in his new red "buff coat" an easy target for Narragansett marksmen. The battle at Great Swamp, the Narragansett winter encampment, procured another 350 captives, 300 of which were women and children.[79]

In the aftermath of this devastating blow to the Narragansett people, Rhode Island deputy governor John Easton recorded that the troops continued to hunt down the surviving indigenous people—many of them elderly men, along with women and children who had escaped the swamp battle—and

> *killed and took prisoners-divers of them, as they were found straggling; and burnt great Numbers of their Wigwams (or Houses)....* [T]*hey solde those Indians they had taken...for slaves...but one old man that was carried of* [f] *our Island upon his suns back he was so decrepid Could not go and*

when the army tooke them upone his back Caried him to the garrison, sum would have had him devoured by doges but the tenderness of sum of them prevailed to Cut ofe his head.[80]

Throughout the war, individual commanders took captives and dealt with them in differing ways. Plymouth's Benjamin Church is said to have offered captives the choice of joining his forces and proving their loyalty by killing or bringing in other Indian prisoners—or being sold out of the colony. While some took him up on the offer, he sent captives throughout the war for processing in Plymouth. In the fall of 1676, Church led a raid on Martha's Vineyard to seek Wampanoag and Narragansett who had fled there.

The soldiers "tooke many captives and brought them to Plymouth" but also took captives for themselves in lieu of payment from authorities, including Church's gift of a nine-year-old boy to the Thatcher family of Hingham.

That same fall, Massachusetts authorities interned many "Christian Indians" who had learned English and worshiped in Puritan fashion on Deer Island in Boston Harbor and Long Island. While the official order stated the need to "protect" those indigenous people who had accepted Christianity, they marched them to the boats roped with yokes around their necks and hands—like slaves.[81]

The Slave Trade from New England

The European victory over the indigenous people would prove to provide money to grow commerce even further, as thousands more captured indigenous people were sent to the West Indies as slaves for the sugar plantations. New slaves were a much-needed commodity, as historian Edmund S. Morgan noted: "Life expectancy in Barbados, especially for the black population, continued to be low throughout the 17th and most of the 18th century. The slaves on Barbados had to be replaced at the rate of about six percent per year."[82] Morgan estimated that between 1640 and 1700, some 169,000 enslaved men, women and children were imported into the British West Indies. By 1700, the Black population had reached about 100,000.

Statistics on the slave populations of individual plantations at various periods yield some idea of settlement size. For the seventeenth century, a randomly collected sample of twenty plantations from 1650 to 1693 gave

Slave market, engraving for Raynal, abbe (Guillaume-Thomas-Francois) publication on the history of the establishment of European influence and commerce in the West Indies, Geneva, 1757. *Courtesy of the John Carter Brown Library at Brown University.*

an average population of 64, ranging from 7 to 150. Some "Negro yards" were even larger: for example, in 1686 Nicholas Abbey had 157 slaves and Antoine Biet claimed that some plantations in 1654 contained from 200 to 300.

Early colonial governors were required to give an account of trade in their colony, addressed to the "Committee on Trade and Plantations" in London. These have provided scholars some authority on the early slave trade in New England, but as government reports go, the numbers were likely greater than reported.

In early December 1638, a ship named the *Desire* from Salem, Massachusetts, slipped into Boston Harbor under the helm of Captain William Pierce. He had brought captured Pequot to the islands of Providence and the Tortugas in the West Indies, and returned, according to Governor John Winthrop, with "salt…tobacco and Negroes."[83]

By 1644, Captain James Smith and Thomas Keiser had convinced three investors in their plan to send three ships to Africa for gold dust and slaves. Only one of the ships is listed as having returned. The *Rainbow* held a cargo of salt, sugar, tobacco and wine, having exchanged the slaves for these goods in Barbados.

Numerous vessels from different owners sailed out of Boston in the coming decades, leading historian Lorenzo Greene to proclaim that "the New England slave trade in the seventeenth century seems to have been centered wholly in Massachusetts." Governor Bradstreet of Massachusetts submitted in 1680 that forty to fifty slaves had been brought into the colony from Madagascar. Most of these were women, whose price ranged from ten to thirty pounds each. In 1696, Governor Samuel Cranston of Rhode Island reported that forty-seven slaves were brought into Newport on a Massachusetts vessel. Of these, fourteen were purchased on the dock for prices ranging from thirty to thirty-five pounds a head.[84] Massachusetts traders profited, as did those from the other colonies, in status, government office and an almost limitless amount of wealth derived from their investments in both land and human chattel.

Just two years before he became governor of the Commonwealth, merchant Jonathan Belcher and four other investors sent the ship *Katharine* to New Guinea, with instructions to the captain to obtain "good likely negroes from 12 to 25 years of age, the greatest part to be boys."[85]

The Faneuils

One of the most iconic sites in the historic city of Boston was constructed by a family intimately linked to the slave trade. The patriarch of the family, Andrew Faneuil, found early success selling slaves from his house, as advertised in the *Boston News Letter* in June 1718. He later built a warehouse where he kept and sold slaves on "Merchants Row." In addition to his shipping empire, Faneuil owned a mansion on Tremont Street, and some £14,000 in stock in the *East India Company*. By the time of his death in 1738, he was the wealthiest man in the city, and much of his wealth and investment in the trade was inherited by his nephew Peter.

The younger Faneuil seemed to relish the trade, writing to his partners in London to obtain five pipes of Madeira wine, adding, "[A]s this wine is for the use of my house, I hope you will be careful that I have the best." He was also particularly finicky about the slaves brought back for his mansion on Beacon Street, writing implicit instructions to his captains to purchase

> *for the use of my house, as likely a straight limbed negro lad as possibly you can, about the age of from 12 to 15 years; and if to be done, one that has had the small pox, who being for my own service, I must request the favor you would let him be one of as tractable a disposition as you can find, which I leave to your prudent care and management; desiring, after you have purchased him, you would send him to me by the first good opportunity, recommending him to a particular care from the captain.*[86]

Faneuil's most notorious endeavor was the journey of the *Jolly Batchelor*, which was attacked by the Portuguese and weathered an onboard uprising but still managed to limp back to port in 1743 with twenty slaves included with the cargo. Peter Faneuil did not live to see its return, as he died of dropsy on March 3, 1743, just six months after his opening of Faneuil Hall, the great marketplace that would later be called the "cradle of liberty."

Cornelius Waldo

Waldo immigrated to Ipswich, Massachusetts, as early as 1645, though he was once reported to comment that he had arrived so early in the colony that the city of Boston contained but seven huts. In 1652, his father-in-law gave him forty-nine acres in Chelmsford Falls, and Waldo continued to accumulate land in Chelmsford and Dunstable, Massachusetts, as his import business continued to expand. He imported such varied goods as "Choice Irish Duck, fine Florence wine, negro slaves and Irish Butter."[87]

His son Samuel Waldo continued the family business, sending the ship *Africa* on numerous voyages across the Middle Passage in the early eighteenth century. On one voyage to the coast of Africa under Captain Rhodes in 1734, the captain purchased two hundred slaves, "a ton of bees wax and a half ton of ivory." A bout of flux among the captive slaves deprived the captain of much of his cargo en route to the West Indies, and he settled for selling the remainder for cocoa.

Waldo balked at payment for the unsalable cargo, and Rhodes sued, eventually winning a settlement in court. A great-grandson of Cornelius Waldo, one Ralph Waldo Emerson, wrote in the early years of the Civil War that "emancipation is the demand of civilization" and urged Congress to end "this mischief of slavery," two years before President Lincoln signed the Emancipation Proclamation.

The Royalls

Isaac Royall Sr. came from humble beginnings in North Yarmouth, now part of Maine. In those early years of settlement, his family uprooted themselves and moved to Dartmouth, Massachusetts, where Royall found success as a merchant trading in rum, sugar and slaves. His success prompted him to move to Antigua, where he began a sugar plantation. He kept ties to New England by his half-ownership in a Massachusetts vessel. His son Isaac Royall Jr. was born in Antigua in 1719.

The plantations there, as with other West Indian plantations, faced drought, hurricanes and, in 1735, an earthquake. A smallpox epidemic and then a slave revolt in 1736 prompted the Royalls to return to Massachusetts. Despite the setbacks during their time in Antigua, the trader's wealth allowed him to purchase a five-hundred-acre estate along the Mystic River he called Ten Hills Farm.

By 1738, Isaac Royall Sr. was advertising "a group of likely Negroes from 10 to 12 years." The sprawling estate included a colonial farmhouse, a stable and carriage house, as well as barns and outbuildings. Some twenty-seven slaves were brought from Antigua for both domestic and field labor on his estate. It is estimated that over a forty-year period, some sixty slaves lived and worked on the Royall estate.

The west façade of the Isaac Royall House, Medford, Massachusetts. *Courtesy of Wikipedia Commons, photo by Daderot 2015.*

Isaac Royall Jr. continued the trade after inheriting the estate and eighteen of the slaves there. He used his wealth and status to attain civic positions, holding the rank of honorary brigadier general in the local militia, serving on the Medford Board of Selectmen, then as representative from the town on the Governor's Council from 1752 to 1774. He was also an overseer of Harvard College, from which he had graduated, and held pews at both Christ Church and Kings Chapel.

Royall also renovated his home, expanding the farmhouse into a three-story Georgian mansion with a new façade. He also extended added a clapboard extension that became the slave quarters. His lifestyle was like that of a planter in his native Caribbean: riding in a luxurious carriage, accompanied by liveried servants, holding lavish parties at which guests would be served dinner on the finest china and relaxing in a home filled with imported furniture and luxurious furnishings, including silver. In the census of 1754, the Royall household listed twelve slaves. He fled Medford at the start of the Revolutionary War, leaving behind his remaining slaves, who were emancipated by the Commonwealth.

Rhode Island's Dominant Role

Rhode Island vessels began fetching slaves for the Caribbean market as early as 1700, according to William B. Weeden: "One ship and two sloops sailed directly from Newport to the African Coast; Edwin Carter commanded the ship and partly owned in the three vessels. With him sailed one Bruster and John Bates, merchants of Barbados, and separate traders from thence to the coast of Africa." All these vessels carried cargoes to Barbados and sold them there.[88]

Economist Samuel Coles noted that Narragansett Bay shipowners were enticed by the highly speculative nature of the trade and that low investment costs, rising demand and profits easily outweighed the risks involved. "By 1740," he wrote, "the Rhode Island trading fleet numbered 120 vessels, many of which were engaged in African slaving operations or in West Indian commerce.…[F]ollowing the abolition of the duty on slaves in 1732, Newport began a meteoric expansion, which, by 1769, made it the principal northern slave market and the most important commercial center of southern New England."[89]

The Trade from Newport

Established in 1639 and soon after a principal port of commerce for the colony, Newport became an island city of immense diversity amid its wharves and dockside counting houses and taverns. Beyond the waterfront district were grandly designed wooden mansions for the merchant families who profited from the bustling commercial trade of all shades.

Historian Elaine Forman Crane noted that the trade developed early on among the more elite families on the island:

> *Newport's participation in the slave trade became noticeable in the 1730's. There were few voyages in that decade, but the people who would take their place among the first families of slaving—the Scotts, Redwoods, Malbones, and Vernons—were among the most active in the trade and while these merchants were joined in the 1740's and 1750's by such notable names as the Bannisters, Cheesebroughs, Ellerys, and Wantons…except for George Rome, Newport's slaving community was limited to longtime residents.[90]*

Shipowners from Rhode Island generally sent their vessels to the Guinea coast, though some were enticed by the higher quality of slaves in Zanzibar and Mozambique despite the longer journey and extended risk. The cargoes were sold in the Caribbean but also in South America and, in some cases, returned to the United States.

John Bours

John Bours was an early Newport merchant who became involved in the slave trade. He operated a store called the Golden Eagle on Cowley's wharf (now Bowen's wharf), where four slaves labored as dockworkers and stocked the store's shelves.

He owned a slaving vessel named the *Newport Pacquet*; it sailed in early May 1763 under Captain Benjamin Hicks. He financed another journey the following year, with additional investments from Thomas Cranston, Isaac Lawton, Captain Hicks and Edmund Furney. This voyage, under Captain James Shearman, transported 172 slaves and arrived in Charleston, South Carolina, on July 8, 1765, with 152 surviving enslaved people.[91]

As late as January 1768, Bours was procuring molasses from other merchants, namely Aaron Lopez & Co. Captain Benjamin Wright penned a letter from Jamaica to keep his employers abreast of the market, warning, "I cannot give any encouragement to send any more Vessels to this island this Year.…Produce will break very high this Year…and if Rum should break high Molasses will be high likewise. In regard to Jno. Bours on Mr. Abraham Lopez in your favor, I have delivered to said Lopez, and received the Bonds in amount of said Order."

In February, he wrote again. To appease the worried merchant, Wright informed Lopez that "shall spare no pains to serve Mr. Bours as I No his necessity," and by March, Wright provided an update from Savana La Marr: "We have now on board the *America* eighty-six hhds Molasses, and shall to morrow send to be filld forty more. Should have been one of the first Ships for home, had not Mr. Bours' order prevented."[92]

By the 1774 census, Bours was listed as being taxed for ownership of two enslaved servants.[93]

The Malbones

During the early period of commerce in slave-related goods, Godfrey Malbone of Newport was lauded as "the most considerable trader of any here to the coast of Guinea." Those words, written by the traveling Scottish physician Dr. Alexander Hamilton in 1742, reveal a visitor somewhat overwhelmed by the world of the planters' lavish lifestyles.

Malbone's mansion was, according to Hamilton,

> *the largest and most magnificent dwelling house I have seen in America. It is built entirely of rough-hewn stone of reddish colour; the sides of the windows and corner stones of the house being painted like white marble. It is three stories high and the rooms are spacious and magnificent.… [R]ound it are pretty gardens and canals and basins for water, from whence you have a delightful view of the town and harbor of Newport.*[94]

The gardens themselves reportedly contained three fishponds, numerous exotic plants, flowers and shrubbery accented with a pink sandstone sundial. Numerous fruit and cedar trees also grew on the estate, a garden of Eden so famous that even after Malbone's mansion burned, visitors came to see the grounds.[95]

Between 1728 and 1738, Godfrey Malbone sent nearly fifty vessels, including sloops, brigs, snows and ships, to destinations such as Antigua, Barbados, St. Christopher, St. Kitts, Nevis, Surinam and Jamaica.

The "invoice of Sundry Merchandise" shipped on the brig *Eagle* on March 31, 1730, includes:

> *11,000 boards*
> *15,000 staves*
> *29,790 shingles*
> *5,500 additional boards*
> *3,800 hoops*
> *23 horses*
> *2 oxen, as well as oats, hay, water, halters, 50 bushels of corn, and 14 gallons of rum and sugar*[96]

The invoice from the brig *Hector*, which sailed that same month, shows that Malbone was sending a variety of horses to Barbados, as his explicit list of the equines and their value shows:

2 White Coach horses	*£70*
2 Bay Stone horses	*65*
2 Black ditto	*60*
2 D[itto] younger, taller	*59*
1 Bay	*36*
1 Black	*20*
1 Sorrel Stone	*19*
1 Black Gelding	*26*
1 Browne Stone	*35*
1 Bay Stone	*30*
1 Browne Stone	*45*
1 Bay Gelding	*33*
1 Black Stone	*24*
1 Bay Gelding	*30*
1 Bay ditto	*20*
1 Gray	*40*
1 D[itto] Gray	*26*
1 Sorrel Stallion	*45*
1 Bay Gelding	*35*[97]

The sloop *Speedwell*, sent to Antigua in July 1733, carried the usual supply of pine boards, staves, hoops and shingles as well as sixteen barrels of menhaden, six barrels of sugar, sixty sheep "had of Mr. Brenton" and fifteen horses, among other goods. Such a lucrative business naturally led to the Malbones' entry into the slave trade.

Godfrey's brother John Malbone began his slaving ventures as early as 1737, the beginnings of a long career as a slaveowner and trader. He survived a tragedy that occurred off Point Judith when a boy dropped a candle into a cask of rum, resulting in an instant conflagration. Before the longboats could be lowered, many passengers perished in the flames.[98]

The brothers developed a scheme for avoiding customs payments by pretending to purchase duty-free molasses in Jamaica, for which a captain was instructed to "get a clearance from the Custom House there for as much molasses as you shall judge your vessel will stow," but then "proceed with your casks full of water for Ballast to Port au Prince," where the captain would find "our Friend John Baptiste La Barthe who will deliver you a cargo of molasses." The captain was instructed to load this and head for Hispaniola "with the greatest Expedition."[99]

In 1764, the brothers inherited a 3,500-acre farm in Pomfret, Connecticut, with an inventory list of 80 cows, 45 oxen, 30 steers, 59 young cattle, 6 horses,

600 sheep, 180 goats, 150 hogs and, listed last of the property, 27 slaves who worked the farm.[100] John Malbone was well known to be a strict overseer. He complained in a letter to his brother of repeated theft committed "by my father's negroes, Jos, Jack, James, and Master Primus.…These fellows have broken open the Mills near the farm three times, stole from thence forty odd bushels of corn meal at different times," and promised Godfrey that the slave Primus would "relate the whole as whipping and imprisonment has made him put on the appearance of honesty at present."

Such cruelty toward slaves seemed inherent within many of the later generations of planters and was remarked on by one of their peers. The young John Dickinson was the son of a wealthy Quaker planter. Rather than choose the lifestyle of a plantation owner, he began to study law and removed himself to London, where he felt he could receive the best education. While there, he wrote of the delusions of grandeur cultivated by the sons of such planters and the "pride, selfishness, peevishness, violence, anger, meanness, revenge, and cruelty" that came from owning and working slaves to their limit. Dickinson believed that such a shallow lifestyle left these young men unprepared to learn and negotiate with their peers in other places, much less in England, where "the first lesson a person learns is that he is nothing."[101]

At this time, the Malbones were considered the largest slaveowners in Connecticut, though it is impossible to discern how many slaves were transported directly there from the islands or between properties in Rhode Island and Connecticut.

The Vernons

William and Samuel Vernon were born in Newport to a local silversmith. As adults, they entered into business together—their first ship said to be named the *Olive Branch*—and ultimately became among the better-known merchants of the town. The brothers owned the sloop *Hare* and the brigs *Reynard* and *Othello* and partnered with numerous owners of other vessels in the triangle trade. William Vernon partnered often with the Redwoods on ventures to Barbados. The brothers partnered also with Thomas Taylor, another Newport merchant whose family roots lay in Virginia. Taylor's son William captained the brig *Royal Charlotte* and the schooner *Little Sally* on ventures for the partnership in 1762. On his return to Newport aboard the *Royal Charlotte*, Captain Taylor had some grim news, printed for all in the *Newport Mercury*:

> The Brig Royal Charlotte *Captain Taylor, arrived here last Thursday from Annamaboe, on the Coast of Africa, after a Passage of 110 Days by whom we have affecting intelligence of the tragical Death of Captain George Frost, by Mr. William Grant, his Mate, both of this Town, which was perpetrated by the Slaves on board his Sloop, as she lay at Anchor in the River Gaboone, in the month of November last.*

The newspaper related the story of how Captain Frost sent two crew members and a slave ashore to collect water and wood and then let a good number of slaves, reportedly about sixty, on deck. He and the remaining crew members were quickly overtaken and thrown overboard. Frost attempted to climb back aboard and was pierced by a lance. He drowned while trying to reach the shore. The enslaved took command of the vessel and fended off another effort to retake the ship, bringing up small arms and barrels of powder onto the deck. A resultant explosion took the lives of some thirty slaves, and the vessel was retaken three days later.[102]

William Taylor continued to sail the *Royal Charlotte* until 1767. On arrival off the African coast, Taylor contacted local agents, including Richard Brew, to acquire the slaves needed for the return voyage. Taylor sailed the brig from Africa to markets in St. Croix and Hispaniola.

The Vernon brothers transported at least 544 slaves to West Indian ports between 1755 and 1774 on their own vessels, with hundreds more undocumented and hundreds of others in partnership with other ship owners. Historian Richard Pares noted, "When a ship owner had two or more vessels plying to the same West Indian port, as Aaron Lopez had in Jamaica and the Browns at Surinam, combinations of this sort favored economy and timing….[I]t is hardly less easy to see why the return cargo ought not to fall short of the vessels capacity."[103]

Aaron Lopez and Jacob Rivera

Lopez, like the Browns of Providence, sent a variety of goods to the West Indies, as evidenced by a listing of the "Sale of Sundrys of the Sloop *Industry* in Barbados in 1769–1770." The list includes forty-four sheep (thirty-seven sold to sundry persons), fourteen horses, oars, foot boards, staves, hoops, shingles, cheese, onions, oil, pickled fish, candles and flour. Crews were relatively small; the crew list of the ship *America* shows that the ship sailed in August 1765 with the Shipmaster Francis Pope, a first and second mate and seven sailors. While such "sundry goods" were the staples of Lopez's voyages, he also dealt directly in slaves.

Between 1761 and 1775, Aaron Lopez, with his father-in-law, Jacob Rivera, consistently financed joint slaving ventures, and between them, the sent twenty slave ships of various types—brigs, sloops, schooners and snows—on twenty-five voyages to such destinations as Africa, Antigua, Barbados and Jamaica.

Lopez and Rivera's brigs were outfitted in the fashion of Rhode Island slavers, an efficient method of human trafficking for its time, though a potential European buyer once deemed one of his ships "remarkably small" and "unsuitable for the trade from Liverpool."[104] On a common vessel, the passageway between the deck and the hold was but a crawlspace, but with a ship used as a slaver, that space was expanded to often four or five feet high with platforms built out from the bulkhead at all sides, midway between the deck and the headway about six feet in length, by which the average ship could accommodate 120–30 slaves.

From 1767 to 1783, Lopez sent the brigs *Sally* and *Cleopatra* to the islands numerous times. A typical cargo aboard the *Sally*, which set out from Block Island for "Som islands in the west Endies" in August 1767, included oxen, sheep and "bucks," barrels of herring and spermaceti and tallow candles.[105] On this voyage, *Sally*'s travels included the Leeward and Turks and Caicos Islands. Captain Nathaniel Briggs was charged with bartering said merchandise for slaves. During this one voyage, he collected 125 slaves.

On his voyages, Briggs bartered for slaves in several ways, sometimes directly with other ship captains at port, at other times with plantation owners and occasionally with shadowy entities such as "a Black Trader" or "a Quaker." In Nevis, for example, he bartered with one John Holman for a "gal slave," a young girl measured at three feet, eight inches tall. Briggs paid with a barrel of rum, two cages of lobsters, "choklat," sugar, onions and tobacco.

Fellow captain Robert Elliot, on the other hand, gave him what was sure to be a bargain, when he sold Briggs another "gal slave" for the price of a barrel of rum, onions, a hat and a pair of shoes.

In another entry, Briggs received six slaves from the governor of St. Croix. In St. Kitts, he delivered sheep, spermaceti candles, tar and turpentine to planters and by October 11 was "bound for Rhode Island."

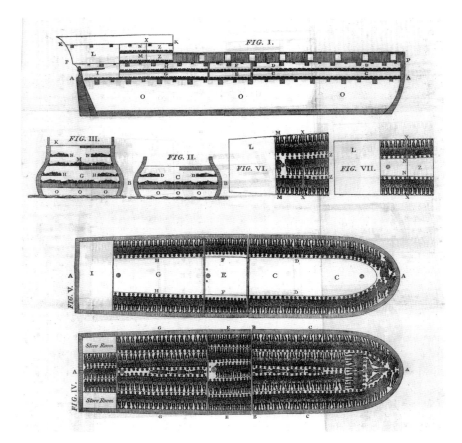

Diagram of a Slave ship, engraving by G. Shulze, London, 1821. *Courtesy of the John Carter Brown Library at Brown University.*

The majority of these enslaved likely ended on southern plantations, where slaves of African origin and slaves like these, brought up on a West Indian plantation, were prized for their skill at handling livestock in an open-range setting, as opposed to the walled or fenced-in pastures of New England.[106] By 1760, Rhode Island vied with North Carolina as one of the busiest slave trading colonies in the world.

Such a bustling trade presented opportunity to nearly every man who owned or had access to a ship, even a common mariner such as Nathaniel Briggs. These early voyages no doubt tested his skills and were met with approval. The mariner from Tiverton would be in Aaron Lopez's employ from 1766 to the outbreak of the Revolutionary War.

The Ventures of Captain Briggs

More common than this voyage on the *Sally* were Briggs's journeys to the coast of Africa, from where he would purchase and transport cargoes of slaves to various destinations in the West Indies. He took the *Sally* to the African coast in 1766–67, transporting 120 slaves to Barbados and St. Kitts. The following year, he sailed the brig *Hannah* to the West Coast of Africa and transported 126 slaves to Jamaica.

Nathaniel Briggs was first named captain of the vessel *Cleopatra* in early 1770, as he recorded in the log on January 13: "At 8 am the morning Came to Sail from the Long Wharf in Newport, Rhode Island the good ship *Cleopatra*…with the wind NNW Bound for Damennica."[107] The ship sailed through snow squalls for the first few days until the weather broke and proceeded without much incident until February 4, when the ship "Maid Island of Domenica." Briggs lingered in the islands that winter, recording in the log again on April1, when he took his departure from Crooked Island in the Bahamas with the company of a "Capt. Tigett of Rhode Island."

Briggs sailed the *Cleopatra* from Newport on July 9, 1770, picking up 108 slaves on the coast, and arrived in Jamaica with 96 on January 11, 1771. In July of that year, he sailed the *Cleopatra* again, leaving Africa with 257 slaves bound for Barbados, and again the following year, transporting 183 slaves to Barbados and Jamaica.

On May 1, 1773, Briggs recorded in his usual jovial style the start of a journey: "At 7 in the Morning drag anker and Came to sail from Newport Rhode Island in the good ship Africa." In February 1774, he noted that "at 3am wayed anker from annamaboe road with the wind at ____and came to sail Bound off the Coast of the West Enges in the good ship Africa…with one hundred and eighty three slaves."[108] On February 11, Briggs recorded that he had "[l]ost a woman slave that was sick which I believe went overboard." On April 4, he recorded that at "half after foure Clock Maid Land Barbados at Eight in the morning Came to anker in Carlmen bay." Illness was still a factor on the vessel. On April 11, in the side margins of his usual reporting of the weather and swells, Briggs noted, "[T]his day buried 1 man slave, 12 in all dead."[109] On July 14, he left the Bahamas bound for Block Island.

In his logbook, Briggs left a picture of what we must assume is a Narragansett Pacer, though dressed as a West Indian planter may have had his horse prepared for riding. It is the sole adornment in an otherwise generally mundane and poorly handwritten record.

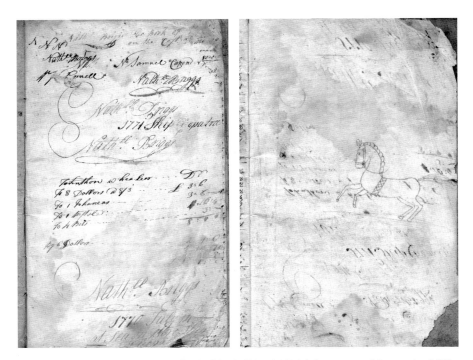

Left: Nathaniel Briggs. Ship's Log Book, Rhode Island 1771 ink on paper. Manuscript MSS 541 BI F3 RHi X17 4271 *Courtesy of the Rhode Island Historical Society.*

Right: Nathaniel Briggs. Ship's Log Book Horse Drawing. Rhode Island 1771 Pencil on paper. Manuscript MSS 541 BI F3 RHi X17 4270. *Courtesy of the Rhode Island Historical Society.*

After the American Revolution, Briggs reemerged as captain (and possible owner) of the *Three Friends* and sailed it from Newport in August 1785, transporting 114 slaves to St. Thomas. The following year he was listed as part owner, or investor, of the brig *Washington*, as well as part owner of the *Three Friends*, with his former employer Jacob Rivera and Co. Briggs also partnered with Caleb Gardner to send the brig *Hope* and the sloop *Dove* on ventures to St. Eustatius and Africa, respectively, in 1777–78.

By March 1789, he was listed as the sole owner of the *Dove*, which sailed that month from Newport and transported 114 slaves from the African coast to an unlisted destination. The following year, he partnered with Gardner again to send the sloop to Havana and the *Hope* to the same port in 1792–93. Briggs took up sponsorship again with Peleg Clarke to sail the *Washington* to Africa in August 1794.

According to statistics compiled by the archivist of the Little Compton Historical Society, Nathaniel Briggs was responsible for "the forced transport of 2,166 enslaved people and the deaths of 267 people during their middle passages from Africa to their points of sale."[110]

Peleg Clarke

Peleg Clarke had his own vessel, the schooner *Nancy*, which he sailed from Newport on small slaving ventures, but he was better known for his skills as a captain.

In 1768, he was listed as Captain and owner of the snow *Whim*, transporting sixty-six slaves to St. Eustatius. Clarke took the same ship on another venture in September of the following year with an equal number of slaves.

He was captain of the ship *Fletcher* in 1773 when it departed Newport for Africa and then sailed Jamaica and London before returning to New England with a cargo of molasses, hemp, canvas and a few crates of tea.[111] He sailed into Boston Harbor on November 27, 1773. Cast into the heart of the erupting riots, he witnessed the sacking of a house belonging to Richard Clarke, the agent of the East India Company, and was subject to threats from the rioters if he or other captains attempted to unload their cargo on the docks. Several weeks later, he managed to unload his tea at a loss and sailed for Newport on December 16.

Peleg Clarke was also listed as captain of the brig *Thames*, which departed from Newport on June 20, 1774, and left the African coast bound for Barbados with 304 slaves. He captained the brig again, departing Newport in October 1775 and leaving the coast of Africa with 279 slaves bound for Jamaica. Off the Cape in late November, an insurrection among the slaves broke out, resulting in the deaths of 31 to 33 slaves.[112] Clarke did not arrive at his destination until April 1777, with 240 slaves.

Early in his career, Clarke also co-sponsored voyages with London agent John Fletcher and later with diverse partners on larger transports, such as the ship *Ascension*, which left Boston and then Newport in mid-October 1791 for Africa, then sailed for Havana with 240 slaves. His next venture, with the brig *Whim*, also listed Audley Clarke as part owner, though Peleg appeared as sole owner that same year of the *Peatt*, which transported small cargoes of slaves to Havana from 1792 to 1794. He was also listed as the sole owner of the *Sally*, which transported 69 slaves to Havana in 1793.

Clarke continued his partnership with Caleb Gardner, William Vernon and Sam Brown in sending the *Ascension* on a venture to Montevideo with 283 slaves in November 1795. He partnered with Audley Clarke to send the *Sally* to St. Kitts, which departed Newport in June 1796 and transported 136 slaves. This appears to have been Clarke's last venture.

Such was the opportunity that the slave trade presented in Rhode Islander that a local mariner could find favor with an owner after years of loyal service or use his own resources and become wealthy enough to invest in other ventures or own a slaving vessel outright.

Jay Coughtry rightly pointed out, however, that these captains who rose to such a level were few and far between. As he wrote in *The Notorious Triangle*, "For most captains…the slave trade did not provide the key to the counting house door."[113]

Most were captains for life on the sea and took orders from owners who wished mainly for expediency in shipping goods, slaves and other cargo to their destinations with a speedy return. Aaron Lopez's letter to Captain William English, assigned to the brig *Ann* for a voyage in November 1772, is an example of a common letter of instruction. Lopez's letter makes clear his business intentions:

> Our orders to you are that you Embrace the first fair wind and make the best of your lay on the Coast of Africa.…[W]e think it advisable, that as soon as you procure the necessary rice that you proceed without delay to Anomosoe Road; when please God you arrive there safe convert your cargo into good Slave; on the best terms you can.[114]

Annamaboe was the largest slaving port on the Gold Coast, and Rhode Islanders were frequent visitors there. Historian Randy Sparks wrote, "The Rhode Island merchants were a fixture at Annamabo." As early as 1736, a Rhode Island captain recorded that there were nineteen ships anchored there, "7 of us Rume [rum] men that are ready to Devur [devour] one another" in the fierce competition for slaves.[115]

On this voyage, owner Lopez gave Captain English some additional business to be concluded:

> We here inclose you David Mill Esq. of Cape coast Castle's receipt for twenty-seven men and thirteen women slaves, left in his hands by Capt. Briggs the last voyage on our accounts payable to his or our order, which we have made payable to you; When you have finished the sale of

your Cargo, apply to the said Mr. Mill and receive from him the above mentioned slaves.

To these slaves we desire you'll put some particular mark that may distinguish them from those of the Cargo, so that their sales in the West Indies may be kept by itself, for the Insurance on these is not blended with the Cargo.[116]

Lopez then instructed Captain English to sail on to Jamaica, proceed directly to Savannah La Mar and there "deliver your whole quantity of slaves on our account to Captain Benjamin Wright in whose hands we shall lodge whatever future orders we may have occasion to give you."

But slaving voyages were not always so cut and dried, and they seldom went as an owner wished when he drew out instructions on pen and paper. The *Ann* arrived at the "Island of Doles" off the Coast [African?] after a voyage of forty days, but problems seemed to plague the venture as soon as English's arrival on "Anamosoe Road."

First, Mill balked at paying for the cargo on any terms, especially with slaves, as "he owing a great many Slaves and Every Ship to take their turn to be paid according to their Contract."[117] When reminded of his obligation for slaves from Briggs's voyage, the governor promised to deliver these before English set sail for Jamaica.

In the letter English wrote to Lopez dated March 10, 1773, he bluntly reported, "Here is very poor times for every fort and private house is stocked with Rum that there is Noe Selling of Rum Nor anything else. I have Not Ben five Nights on board since my arrival but Continually Cruising from one fort to another." English was able to strike a deal at a considerable loss, but, as he wrote, "These are the only terms I could sell any part of the Cargo and I find that the Market grows worse instead of grown better."

By May he was still attempting to sell his cargo for slaves—and had collected thirty—but wrote of another setback for the venture caused by a "worthless Drunking fellow of a Chief Mate," who, dispatched in the long boat to Cape Cord with "Twenty Three water casks, Two Barrls flour one Box Soap and fifty lbs of Coffee," apparently drank so much that as he approached the shore, "Carrying more sail than Good Judgement would allow him…took in a Large Quantity of water and stood so nigh the Shore that he was almost in the Breakers, whereupon the Natives perceveing came off with a number of Cannoes."

When the natives boarded the longboat, it was overset, with "Every Shillings worth lost" of the goods the mate was to deliver for gold. By the first week of June, English had collected forty slaves but was still waiting on the slaves Mill had promised him. On July 12, 1773, Mill wrote directly to Lopez and Jacob Rivera:

> *Gentlemen;*
>
> *I received by Captain English your favor also sundry stock for shipping of which I am greatly obliged to you. I have been only able, trade being so bad to pay Captain English 30 of the 40 slaves I owed Capt. Briggs last voyage, but I shall pay him the remainder and hope the detention of those 10 will be no loss to you. If it is I will thankfully pay you.*[118]

English left the coast of Africa mid-July with a bill of lading for thirty slaves, "in good order and well-conditioned" marked distinctly, as Lopez had directed: "19 men slaves, marked 'O' on the right thigh, and 11 women marked ditto. Being part of the ship 'Cleopatra's' cargo left by Capt. Nath. Briggs the last voyage to Africa."

A separate bill of lading listed an additional thirty-three male slaves, twenty-seven women, two boys and three girls, totaling ninety-five slaves that

Shackles from a Rhode Island slave ship. *Courtesy of the John Hay Library at Brown University.*

the *Ann* carried from the coast of Africa. After a passage of eighty-five days, English arrived in Kingston, Jamaica, with eighty-nine slaves, having "had the misfortune of Buriing Six Slaves on my Passage."

Misfortune continued for the slaves, and the owner's pockets, for no sooner had he arrived than a strange swelling disorder began to appear among the captives. This "first Begun in their feet and worked upward when Gott as far as their Stomach they Dyed in a few hours."[119] So rapidly did the illness become "so Violent among the Slaves, that Nine of them was sold for a mere trifle and had not the whole Being sold in a few Days I believe I should Lost one half of the whole."

In January, he wrote to Lopez that he had obtained molasses, but that "at what price the Remainder of the Cargoe will be purchased for is uncertain at present, Every kind of Northward produce is a Glut here att present and Beares a poor price." Nonetheless, he departed for Newport later that month with a cargo of eight thousand gallons of molasses.

The Champlins

One of Lopez and Rivera's chief rivals in trade from Newport was Christopher Champlin (1731–1805). Champlin was the son of Colonel Christopher Champlin, who had moved the family from Newport to Narragansett Country and became a fairly prominent planter in the region, using his sloop *Patience* to trade with the West Indies from 1732 to 1738. His sons, however, all returned to Newport to begin their careers.

Christopher and his brothers George and Robert worked together from Newport on numerous trading ventures. Like the Malbones, they utilized sloops, brigs, ships and snows to trade with Jamaica, Monte Cristi, Antigua and Tortola, among other ports. The brothers dabbled in privateering as well as "victualizing"—sending provision vessels to the French during the French and Indian and Revolutionary Wars. Their ventures included slavery, which proved profitable for the family. Christopher and George financed most of the ventures, with George often also serving as master aboard the slave vessel. Between 1769 and 1775, their slaving ventures averaged a return of nearly £1,000 sterling per voyage.[120]

The Champlins used their sloop *Adventure* for several slaving ventures to Barbados between 1770 and 1774 and also sent the sloop to St. Eustatius on at least one voyage. They were also frequent visitors to Annamaboe, but when prices fluctuated, were not averse to venturing elsewhere for a greater profit. They further cut expenses by paying crews low wages and taking part of those wages in clothing provided for and during the voyage. Such conditions would have only been tolerated by the inexperienced or those mariners who were in little position to turn down the chance of work. A venture in 1773–74 captained by Robert Champlin included among the crew of ten a "mulatto seaman" named Ephraim Neves, and John Warwick, an Indian, who served as the cook.

Arriving in Sierra Leone in late December, Champlin began bargaining for slave and bought one woman from the Dutch Mining Company for "1 tun of rice." On February 4 in Annamaboe, he exchanged another 140 gallons of rum for a female slave. The *Adventure* loitered off the coast through March until the most profitable trade came at Cape Coast near the end of the month, with Champlin purchased thirty slaves between the twenty-first and thirtieth for 7,512 gallons of "rum brought down." At the end of April, back in Annamaboe, he exchanged rum for nine more slaves, as well as "guinea stuff" and "fish for the slaves." May 1 saw another large wholesale purchasing of human cargo: sixteen more slaves for an average of 200 gallons of rum each. Between May 18 and June 10, the crew lost three men and one female slave, whom they buried in Granada. The cargo was delivered in St. Eustatius, and the ship was back at harbor in Newport in July 1774. Robert served as captain of the *Adventure* on another venture in November of that year, to transport a collected 103 slaves, arriving in Jamaica nearly a year later with 92 slaves in cargo.

It has been written that all of the Champlins were members of the Fellowship Club, a social organization whose membership was "made up entirely of slave ship captains and included some of the more notorious Newport slavers such as Abraham Ali, Peleg Clarke, Caleb Gardner, John Jepson, Robert Stoddard, and Joseph Wanton."

With the onset of the Revolutionary War, the Champlins fled Newport. Christopher Champlin engaged in trade through his "victualizing" vessels, and at least one of his slaves from home, also known as Robert Champlin, enlisted in the First Rhode Island Regiment to earn his freedom. George Champlin served as an officer in the Rhode Island Continentals for the duration of the war.

The temptations of imagined fortune in the trade were far-reaching and often risky for those less well-connected families. Rhode Islander William Grant sailed to Annamaboe aboard the *Friendship* from Newport in 1762, intending to establish himself in business at the port. He found "times here very indifferent here" and decided to take a job at Castle Brew, the large and luxurious trading post attached to a British military fort. While he may have felt that he had found a job in paradise, he lingered only three months as a clerk before his death.[121]

John Bannister

John Bannister became one of the most prominent merchants in Newport during the most active years of trade. Being from a wealthy London merchant family gave him an advantage: his father had immigrated to Boston and was successful there, but his adaptation of the New England practices of smuggling and privateering financed his rise in legitimate business. Bannister's marriage to Hermione Pelham of the well-established Newport family greatly increased his landholdings in the city and his status in the community as well. He was able to construct his own wharf, along which he built a counting house and shops in which to sell the goods he imported.

He built a Georgian manor house on Pelham Street, constructed between 1748 and 1751, which at the time was surrounded by acres of meadows and orchards but offered an unobstructed view of the harbor. Bannister also owned two large farms in Middletown, each holding about 150 acres, where he grew produce, raised livestock and made cider.

Research by Marian Mathison Desroisiers showed that the merchant and his co-owners were sailing vessels early to the South with goods, sending the *Benjamin* to South Carolina in February 1739 and the *Hermione* on three voyages to Charleston between 1740 and 1744. Another eight ships stopped at southern ports on their way to London or Holland over the next seven years.

The merchant's business brought all manner of goods to Bannister's Row, including textiles, home goods, hardware and slaves. It is uncertain when he entered the slave trade, but one historian attributed his entry into the market from a letter written to Bannister by Liverpool merchant Joseph Manesty in 1747, informing him of the profit to be made in the trade. He had sent a vessel out the year before with a cargo that cost him £1,800 pounds. The slaves accrued from the trade of that cargo realized some £13,000 in St. Kitts. Bannister could not turn his back on such profit.

A page from his account book of 1746–49 shows that his vessels were outfitted for such trade. His expenses show that he employed a Captain John Brown, as well as a brewer, butcher, bricklayer, brazier, two coopers and three wharf laborers. Again, research by Desrosiers reveals that eighteen vessels, outfitted, built or owned by Bannister between 1747 and 1749 made

John Bannister House, Newport, Rhode Island. *Photo by the author.*

voyages to Antigua, Jamaica, the Leeward Islands, the Bay of Honduras, St. Kitts and Surinam.[122]

During this period, Bannister purchased one or two slaves per voyage that were brought back for sale in New England. His "Account of Negroes" in his ledger shows that from August 1747 to January 1749, he purchased "a Negro boy named Fortune" from Surinam when he encountered the schooner *Success* and then later sold the same boy to Samuel Aborn in Connecticut for £50 profit, less 10 percent the commission Aborn had paid him before the voyage. In December 1747, he purchased "a Negro man named Cesar" from Captain Charles Bardin, paying £340, and on January 24, 1749, purchased "2 Negro men" for £400 while in the Bay of Honduras from Captain William Warner of the brig *Abigail*.[123]

By 1752, he was advertising the sale of slaves in the *Boston Post* as the "finest cargo of negro men, women, and girls ever imported into New England." The *Post* advertised the sale at his wharf in Newport, but the lot were sold to a Nathaniel Johnson of Guilford, Connecticut, for a price that was likely much higher than Bannister would have realized in Newport.[124]

Rhode Island's Other Slave Ports

The slave trade outside of the famed city also rose precipitously through the eighteenth century, with Providence, Bristol and Warren being the most active ports engaged in the traffic.

The Brown family brought back a handful of slaves to Providence to serve as domestic servants in the mansions built on the hills above the riverfront. By 1733, James Brown and his brother Obadiah were shipping cargo on a regular basis to the West Indies as well as in coastal trade with the southern ports. The latter's son wrote, "My father's books show eight vessels that he had management of…all West Indian vessels."[125]

At least one of these vessels transported slaves. The equipment aboard the *Mary* bound for New Guinea in 1738 included "35 pare of handcuff" to bound the slaves the captain would purchase for sale in the West Indies. After James Brown's death in 1739, his son James Brown Jr. continued the business, mostly trading with the southern ports. He died at sea aboard his sloop *Freelove* in 1751, and it was his large inheritance and the distillery he established in Providence that would propel the second generation of Brown brothers into the slave trade. Twenty years after the voyage of the *Mary*, the brothers, along with investors, dispatched the schooner *Wheel of Fortune* to the African coast with rum to exchange for slaves. In 1764, they outfitted the disastrous voyage of the *Sally*.

The ninety-ton vessel departed from Providence under Shipmaster Esek Hopkins bound for the Windward coast of Africa. On arrival, Hopkins found that his cargo of rum only added to the glutted market, and the price of slaves was greater than anticipated. For nine months, the ship sat off the coast while the shipmaster struggled to fill the hold with human cargo.

So long was the wait and such were conditions on board that nineteen of the purchased slaves died before Hopkins even set sail for the West Indies. During the first week out from Africa, another four slaves died—three of them children—and the remaining slaves attempted an uprising, which was repelled violently.

The remainder of the journey saw continued death, with the slaves still held so dispirited that Hopkins recorded "some drowned themselves, some starved, and others sick & dyed." Those who survived were so emaciated that they brought a poor price. In all, sixty-eight enslaved Africans died during the voyage. The disaster deterred most of the brothers from further direct involvement in the trade, though the distillery supplied voyages of other traders from Providence. John Brown continued the trade with his vessels, financing at least four slave ventures to Africa, including the *Sutton* in 1769. He famously defended the trade and battled his brother Moses, who had become a staunch abolitionist, in court. Later traders from Providence included Captain Cyprian Sterry, who outfitted twenty-three vessels for the trade through 1794.

From the mid-eighteenth century, Bristol's shipping was dominated by the Potter and later DeWolf families, who were related by marriage, beginning when Mark Anthony DeWolf married the sister of his employer Simeon Potter. The Potters sent their first slaving vessels out in 1736 and 1738 with Nat Potter sailing ships to Africa. His son Simeon sent the schooner *King George* on a slaving venture to Monte Cristi in 1764 and dispatched the aptly named sloop *Prosperity* to Barbados in 1767. The following year, he shipped the *King George* once again from Bristol and transported 230 slaves to Dominicas.

Mark Anthony DeWolf captained the *Prosperity* for the first time in January 1769, taking the sloop to the coast of Africa and then to Hispaniola before returning to Rhode Island just a few days past a full year of his departure. A second voyage occurred under his command in 1770–71. He continued to captain his father-in-law's vessels right up to the outbreak of war, sailing the brig *Africa* to Jamaica in 1774–75. Mark Anthony, as with many captains, did not make a fortune, but he left his sons Charles, William, John and especially James well groomed to make their own.

James DeWolf served a maritime apprenticeship during the war and assumed his first command of a slave ship at nineteen, sailing the brig *Providence* for the firm of Brown & Francis from Providence in December 1786. DeWolf also cut his teeth in the trade by serving as captain aboard the schooner *Nancy*, a vessel owned by Samuel Wardell of Bristol.

Meanwhile, his brother John began his own career with the firm in 1785, serving as captain aboard the brig *Enterprise*, which would transport 114 slaves to St. Eustatius. In August 1787, he took the brig on a repeat journey, this time with brother Charles DeWolf listed as the owner. In September 1789, he captained the *Nancy*, now owned by Shearjashub Bourne, on a small slaving venture but from then on remained firmly on the decks of the family-owned vessels. He captained the brig *Nancy* to Havana (1790–91) and the took snow *Sukey* to the same port in 1792–93, but abandoned slaving for farming as soon as his fortune was made.[126]

William DeWolf also climbed the rigging of the slave ship pecking order, partnering with Caleb Garder of Newport as co-owner and captain of the sloop *Betsey* and transporting 99 slaves to St. Martin in 1789–90. He sailed the brig *Sally* on a venture that brought 120 slaves to St. Thomas in 1791–92.

Portrait of James DeWolf
from *Commerce of Rhode Island
1726–1800. Massachusetts
Historical Society.*

By this time, a third generation of sons and nephews were apprenticing for the family firm, and in 1792 alone, the DeWolfs sent five slave vessels—the *Sukey*, the *Nancy*, the sloop *Diana*, the *Sally* and the brig *Patty*—on partnered ventures from Bristol. James DeWolf emerged as the patriarch of this generation and carried the family trade firmly into the nineteenth century, even after the import of slaves became illegal in 1808.

When a DeWolf schooner, the *Lucy*, was impounded on suspicion of illegal activity in 1799, James DeWolf responded through political connections and was able to get Charles Collins—a slave vessel owner and DeWolf captain—appointed customs collector of the port. For the next twenty-two years that Collins held his post, DeWolf slavers fitted out in Bristol as if the trade were legal.[127]

DeWolf acquired sugar plantations in Cuba and transported slaves there, having ready marketable goods when prices were high and a higher workforce when the market was weak. The molasses produced in Cuba by his slaves was shipped to Bristol and loaded onto DeWolf vessels bound for the African coast. Slaves were kept captive in his large stone warehouse as well and listed with the inventory of other marketable goods.

James's nephew George DeWolf continued the trade, dispatching slaver after illicit slaver while building his own luxurious mansion in town. James DeWolf, now a congressman, fended off restrictive measures that would have ended their illicit trade in Bristol, and it was not until Collins was ousted in 1820 that the family's slaving ventures were effectively brought to an end.

Right: Detail from the DeWolf stone warehouse on Bristol Harbor, Bristol, Rhode Island. *Photo by the author*.

Below: The mansion of George DeWolf, who continued the family's involvement with the trade. Bristol, Rhode Island. *Photo by the author*.

The fields of Touissett, where the enslaved worked the farms. This section is now an Audubon Sanctuary. *Photo by the author.*

The village of Warren's slave traders sailed most often with slaves to North America's southern ports, as the reader will learn more of later in this narrative. In 1789, however, the partners in these ventures joined Lee Maxwell and Captain Christopher in financing the voyage of the *Abigail*, which sailed from Warren on September 24 and purchased sixty-four slaves on the African coast. Eleven died on the return voyage.

Slaves brought directly into Warren were engaged in labor on the numerous shipyards on the waterfront, as well as those on the Kickemuit River at the mouth of Mount Hope Bay. The nearby farms of Touisett, as the land there is called, held many slaves as field hands and domestic workers. Through the years of the trade, an estimated one hundred enslaved men, women and children lived within the town.

The Slave Trade in Connecticut

Though there is mention of slaves in Hartford and New Haven as early as the mid-seventeenth century, there was little activity or interest in importing slaves during most of the period. As with the other colonies, the shift from indigenous slaves to those imported from Africa began early. Those who wanted slaves could easily procure them from Massachusetts slavers, and as prices for a slave in Connecticut in 1680 were higher than in the other New England colonies, some undoubtedly found it a worthwhile venture.[128]

Despite the willingness of a few to pay higher prices for slaves, discrimination against Black people either free or enslaved dominated colony policy, with free Black residents and indigenous men forbidden on the streets after nine o'clock at night. The enslaved were forbidden to leave towns without written permission from their masters. In 1717, New London voted to ban free people of color from living in the town or owning land. Such restrictions kept the free Black population relatively low, with only seven hundred listed in the 1730 census.[129]

By mid-century however, slavery had increased considerably, with New London County holding the largest number of slaves in the colony. The county's growth in industry and in agriculture with the rise of large plantation farms worked by slaves precipitated the rise of slavery. On the eve of the American Revolution, Connecticut held New England's largest slave population.[130] As historian Lorenzo Greene noted in his work on African Americans during the colonial period, "Any estimate of the number of slaves per family, would be conjectural. The number ranged anywhere from one to sixty, depending on the affluence and business of the owner."[131]

Connecticut dragged its feet on freeing slaves. Through several motions from 1777 through 1784, the assembly came to vote for gradual emancipation. Still, as late as the 1790 census, a considerable number of farmers, industrialists and individuals owned more than a few slaves. In Greenwich, David Bush still owned eight slaves, and Moses Husted enslaved seven. In Easton, Daniel Shelton listed eight slaves in the census; Agar Judson had six. In New Fairfield, Ebenezer Taylor owned seven slaves. Timothy Hale of Glastonbury owned nine slaves, as did John Hendrick of Windsor. In Norwalk, the Davenports still held sixteen slaves between brothers James and John, but the largest single slaveowner in the census was Philip Mortimer of Middletown, who held eleven slaves.[132]

Plantations along the Connecticut River Valley provided livestock, farm products, lumber and other goods to the West Indies in return for molasses, salt, sugar and slaves.[133] The rising traffic in the triangle trade also brought an increase in shipbuilding on the Connecticut River. An industry that began in Middletown as early as 1669 flourished with the incoming tide of trade, and by the mid-eighteenth century, the town boasted three shipyards on the river.

As a port, Middletown's maritime neighborhood stretched some forty-seven acres. According to historian Erik Hesselberg, "In this seafaring community stood 200 houses, including elegant mansions of merchants and sea captains," including "the beautiful riverfront mansion of Philip Mortimer, with its avenue of buttonwood trees leading down to the water."

At least two offices of slave traders existed in town during this period. In 1756, the town's population of slaves had reached 218, with most families holding a pair of slaves for domestic service. Many others of that population worked in the shipyards or related industry, as did the dozen slaves owned by Philip Mortimer who labored in his prosperous ropeworks at the North End of the district.[134] In this way, slaves labored so that the trade would continue, as would the leisurely lives of their owners here in New England and planters in the West Indies.

The Alsop Family

Richard Alsop Jr. (1627–1776) learned the mercantile trade from Philip Livingston, a successful trader in Manhattan with the East Indies. In 1750, Livingston sent Alsop to Middletown to establish a branch of the firm. Within a few years, he had established his own mercantile store, Alsop & Company, and trade in the more lucrative Caribbean market.

Richard married Mary Wright in 1760, and over the next sixteen years, she bore him ten children. During that time, the Alsops grew wealthy from the West Indian trade. They constructed a mansion on Main and Court Streets in the center of Middletown, and Alsop established a gin distillery and ropeworks in the district. His unexpected death in 1776 left a will of some fifty pages, with an estate valued at over £35,000. He also held a large sum of money in Jamaica, and his inventory listed five domestic slaves.

Alsop's younger brother Joseph Wright Alsop would take up the seafaring end of the business after events prompted the deceased Alsop's partner to flee to England. Though the trade with the West Indies lessened during the American Revolution, Mary Alsop shrewdly increased imports of sugar and molasses for the family distillery in Middle Haddam, as well as mahogany, satinwood and spices. By the 1790s, the Alsop trading house was advertising its prime import as Jamaican rum "sold by the hogshead or barrel," an early indicator of the growth of such commerce.

In the coming decades, vessels would register cargos at the customhouse consisting of as many as 125 casks of rum. In 1820, some 165,000 gallons of rum were imported into Middletown. Such was the commerce that rum became a medium of exchange. The builders of the first courthouse in Middletown were paid in rum, and the liquor was used for the purchase of slaves as well.[135]

Elijah Hubbard

Hubbard was another experienced trader with the West Indies, reaching success before the war and then turning his ships and merchant house to the war effort, serving as a commissary for the Continental army. Many merchants' sacrifices for the war effort paid off, and Hubbard was soon a wealthy man.

He founded Middletown's first chartered bank in 1799 and, in the following year, sailed a new brig named the *Mary* to the Caribbean. Built in Chatham across the river, the 75-ton vessel measured 62.6 feet along the waterline with a beam of 21 feet. The ship was loaded with one thousand hoops, two thousand staves and twenty barrels of pork and beef along with corn, peas, potatoes and oats—all staples for the slaves on the West Indian plantations. The *Mary* also carried fifty-eight head of cattle on deck, while below, twelve tons of hay were stored to feed them on the journey. Hubbard suffered a rare loss with the venture, however, when the *Mary* was seized by French privateers.[136]

The Hallams

Nicholas Hallam came to New London from a prosperous trading family established in Barbados. He married Sarah Pygan in 1686 and, as she was an only child, inherited some £2,000 on her father's death in 1701, allowing Nicholas to build a warehouse, wharf and dock for his vessel. When he died at age forty-nine in 1714, his inventory included "a fine house valued at L275 with its barn, well, and one-and-a-half-acre lot," stores of rum and molasses, 126 ounces of silver and one Black woman. His son Edward had two sons, John and Robert Hallam, who became prosperous merchants at the latter end of the century.

Though in the shadow of the fleets of slave ships that departed and returned to Rhode Island, Connecticut slavers competed with them and European traders along the African coast. While the British raid on New London in 1781 destroyed the decades of shipping records in the customhouse, those that survive attest to a lively engagement in the trade. The logbook recording the voyage of the snow *Africa* from 1757 to 1758 was only recently discovered by historians, and it "reveals that men from the colony were regularly in Africa, buying men, women, and children…transporting captives to the West Indies and back to the American colonies."[137]

A Surinam Planter in His Morning Dress, hand-colored engraving by William Blake, London, 1793. *Courtesy of the John Carter Brown Library at Brown University.*

Anne Farrow's work in unraveling the mystery behind the logbook after its discovery led to yet another link to a pair of patriarchal New England families. The logbook was written in the neat, elegant hand of Dudley Saltonstall, who at eighteen years of age was the supercargo for his father's vessel. Gordon Saltonstall was a deputy and merchant of New London. His family line went back to links with the Saltonstalls, Dudleys and Winthrops of Massachusetts.[138]

Captain John Easton was a descendant of the prominent Rhode Island family, and by the time of the *Africa*'s sailing, when he was thirty-nine, he was a veteran of slaving ventures. As early as 1746, Easton had purchased a lot at the foot of Ferry Street in Middletown. He built a gambrel-roofed mansion and lived there with his wife, Sarah Ward Easton. The captain spent thirty-five years at sea. Later slave traders in his wake brought fortune to the river port. All the mansions of Middletown, like Easton's house, and later entrepreneurs in enslavement were built on profits from the triangle trade.

What of New Haven, Bridgeport and other Connecticut coastal towns?

While records are scarce, among the listings in *Voyages: The Atlantic Slave Trade Database*, we find one Captain Joseph Miller who sailed the *Levant* from New Haven to Senegambia in 1762, delivering slaves to Guadeloupe. He also sailed a ship whose name was not recorded to Sierra Leone in the following year and returned to the slave port in 1764 aboard the *Adventure*.

Dr. Norman Morison immigrated to Hartford, Connecticut, from Scotland after studying medicine in Edinburgh and married a well-to-do widow around 1731. By 1741, he had found success in the mercantile trade rather than the medical profession. His wealth allowed him to accumulate some 1,500 acres of land that included lots in Elington, Hartland, Waterbury and Windsor. He also owned a farm in Bolton. When Morison died in Hartford in 1762, his estate included an extensive library of books in Dutch, Latin and French, some seventy-four pamphlets and three dictionaries. Morison held eleven domestic slaves. According to his inventory, these consisted of four girls, three boys, an old man, his wife and child and another girl, listed separately. He left cash and silver valued at £98, as well as 793 gallons of rum, a far more valued commodity. When he died, the sloop of which he was part owner lay full of cargo in the harbor as well, with "no less than thirty-one slaves valued at £867, including eleven girls and nine boys described as 'sundry new Negroes being 7/16 part Schooner Cargo from Africa.'"[139]

Later Connecticut slavers included the *Polly*, sailed by one Captain Needham to the Gold Coast in 1791. Captain William Van Deursen was also active late in the trade. A shipmaster who represented several merchant houses, he was shipmaster on the *Concord* out of New London in July 1798, when he received his instructions from investors to sail "with all possible dispatch" to the French island of Martinique. Once there, he was instructed to sell the cargo and the ship. If he was unable to make a satisfactory sale, he was to "vest your property in New Negroes and proceed to Havanah, [and] there dispose of your slaves to best advantage." If Havana proved unprofitable, he might try St. Thomas, the instructions suggested, "always having in mind the grand object of profit, which will be the basis of all your arrangements."[140]

A Shift in Trade

In spite of the prohibitions imposed by British, French and Spanish authorities during the course of several revolutionary wars, "Narragansett Bay Captains experienced little difficulty in smuggling cargoes into West Indian ports." For many merchants, the shift came not of any moral quandary but rather concern for their investments, which were threatened by an uprising in Haiti. Christopher Champlin received the news from Benjamin Bailey, who wrote from Port au Prince on December 26, 1791:

> *I arriv'd here this day have horrid News to tell you. The greater part of this place was consumed by fire on the 3rd Inst. and it is now in the greatest confusion. Nothing sells except Poultry and Lumber, all communication between town and Country stop'd and no expectation of a Reconciliation between them very soon....Over 2000 Mulatoes encamped within 9 miles of this place. Last night 150 Troops were landed from on board a frigate lately from France....I shall sail immediately for St. Marc. Intend trying to sell some of my Cargo.*[141]

By the 1790s, the Browns and other Providence merchants had put their risky and often problem-plagued slaving ventures behind them and entered the China trade. John Brown sent the ship *George Washington* to the East Indies on its first voyage in 1787. The ship was to make subsequent voyages for the Browns in 1791 and 1793 and presaged an active period for Providence merchants and the East India trade.

Edward Carrington of Providence was chief among these merchants. Carrington arrived in Providence as a young man from New Haven, Connecticut, and worked as a clerk and later supercargo for several Providence merchants. By 1803, he had been appointed as American consul to

Portrait of Edward Carrington from *Commerce of Rhode Island 1726–1800*. *Massachusetts Historical Society*.

Canton, China, acting as agent for American merchants and amassing a considerable fortune with his own trading ventures, shipping mainly "China goods" to various ports. Three years later, Carrington was in financial straits.

His agent William Lees wrote to inform him of the fluctuating prices of goods on the pages following a list issued in May 1806 of "Liverpool Price Current for American Exports":

> *The late political movements upon the continent & more especially those of Prufour, added to the measures adopted by our Government in consequence, have materially added to the general depression previously felt in our Markets; &, owing to the suspension which has followed in the shipments of West Indies produce to the north of Germany, the prices, now greater, of these articles, are to be considered merely nominal, & I apprehend will so continue until some new & more favorable direction is given to public affairs in that quarter.*[142]

Lees continued,

> *The low prices of Cotton have induced buyers to come forward & some considerable sales have lately been effected at the present quotation....Flour & grain on the other hand...have had a sudden rise, & the prices now stated are fully maintained & expected to improve...of Dyewoods and*

Mahogany, the stocks on hand are very considerable & demand being very limited scarcely support present prices. Rice finds buyers as it arrives at the rates now stated.[143]

Carrington learned from Benjamin Hoppins that the goods shipped on his vessel *Hancock* "came to hand in good order" though "the decline of our markets for Canton goods…we are now sorry to observe that little else can be said, in fact for four months past almost any description of merchandise has remained on hand undemanded—except for home consumption…the consequence of this has been the gradual reduction of prices."[144]

The following June, he received another letter from Hoppins informing him that "although teas are nominally a little higher than they have been a greater price cannot be obtained excepting for a chest or two at a time." That missive informed Carrington of an even greater concern: "Benjamin [?] Clifford mentioned to our [?] the other day the situation of your property on the Coast of Africa. It requires immediate attention or it will be lost and in a very short time our African trade will be entirely at an end and your demand as we understand is payment in slaves."[145]

Carrington's property was likely a holdout from an old investment in the trade. Well into middle age, despite all his advantages, Carrington seemed reluctant to invest heavily in any one venture or to invest in his own. He eventually partnered with Samuel Westmore and found successful trade with Cádiz and the East Indies.

By the first decade of the nineteenth century, a brisk re-export trade of goods from the West Indies to the Baltic regions brought more ships from New England. Historian Stephen Chambers noted, "In 1809-1810 a solid majority of United States vessels arriving in the Baltic hailed from New England." Havana sugar was the most popular re-exported cargo, though minister to Britain John Adams attempted to convince officials the sugar was from Louisiana and Georgia.

Conversely, during the same period, 35 percent of vessels arriving in all of New England were of Cuban origin. Individual ports hosted a high percentage of Cuban vessels, such as those of Bristol and Warren, Rhode Island, where 75 percent of vessels flew the nation's colors; Newport, with its more diverse harbor, still welcomed 45 percent of vessels from the island.[146] Havana then became the prime slave market in the Caribbean, largely because officials ignored Spanish edicts, but Rhode Island vessels also traded in South American ports, chiefly Montevideo and Buenos Aires.[147]

A View of the Harbour and City of The Havana, Taken from Jesu Del Monte, engraving by Elias Dunford, London, 1768. *Courtesy of the John Carter Brown Library at Brown University.*

Slave ships from as far north as Maine contributed to the market, transporting nearly seventeen thousand enslaved individuals to the island. Traders from Maine also colluded with slave traders in Brazil, with at least one notorious Brunswick-built brig, the *Porpoise*, chartered for a year by the slave trader Manoel Pinto de Fonesca out of Rio de Janeiro.[148]

As these shifts were occurring, trade from New England and the West Indies faced a steady decline. The direct trade especially suffered, as entries in the Port of Providence from the West Indies decreased from an average of seventy-four vessels per year between 1791 and 1796 to fewer than forty-eight per year between 1816 and 1830, resulting in a revenue loss of nearly $18,500 per annum.

Those vessels that did transport goods were often undermanned to lower the risk and certainly of no small risk to the average ordinary seaman, as Revolutionary War veteran Samuel Smith discovered when he signed on to numerous vessels after the war. He first signed on a whaling vessel but lost money, returning to Providence with only three hundred barrels of oil. Smith next signed on board a brig bound for the West Indies "four days after my arrival home....Here I began a wickedness beyond anything I had ever done before."

Smith found the voyage "long and tedious"; after picking up a load of salt in New York, they headed for the Turks Islands. Once at sea, the crew found that provisions were very scarce: "Being 18 days from Curago, we were nearly destitute of bread and water, and four days previous to arriving at Turks Island, were obliged to come on an allowence of half a pint of water and half a biscuit a day."[149]

In December 1785, he signed on to a sloop bound to the West Indies, only to find that the "crew consisted of a captain, mate, and four hands—all drunkards except a lad of about eighteen years and myself. We had on board ten oxen."[150] According to Smith, "The captain and mate kept half-drunk the whole voyage. They were not even capable of managing the vessel… when we hauled out into deep water to sail for home, the captain was hardly capable of giving orders."[151]

The task of handling the vessel fell to Smith. Having words with the captain after this incident caused him further trouble. After lying in port for two weeks, they loaded the sloop with cotton and sugar and cleared out for Providence. The animosity between the captain and Smith remained, however, and he described one frightening ordeal that occurred on the journey home:

> *A few days out, our studding sail halyards gave way at the end of the boom where it was rigged out at the end of the yard. The captain called upon me to go aloft and reef the halyards. There was no footrope to rest the feet upon, but I had to crawl out on the yard with the halyards in my hand. When I had got about half way out, the captain sung out with an oath, "now fall overboard, and I will pick you up when I come this way again." I was obliged to cling to the spar to the utmost of my strength, and had it not been for the stillness of the wind and the smoothness of the sea, should have fallen off.*[152]

There were also numerous political factors that affected shipping. Rebellion on St. Dominic in 1791 and fears of other uprisings led to the French Decree of Abolition in 1794. That act alone inspired abolitionists abroad and at home in America, including southern New England, Rhode Island especially, with its large population of Quaker merchants and industrialists, to slowly extract themselves from the slave trade and set emancipation in progress. Meanwhile, some began to grow even wealthier with factories that manufactured rough "slave cloth" from cotton picked by slave labor and then returned for them to wear in the fields of the southern plantations.

The Quasi-War with France between 1795 and 1797—in which American merchant ships were taken by French military vessels—left many ports in the West Indies empty and the plantations on land suffering for supplies. The British navy also had a penchant for boarding American vessels and taking off any seaman of British, Irish or Scottish descent and impressing them into royal service—a life Samuel Johnson likened to being thrown into prison, with a chance of drowning. The Jeffersonian embargo of 1807 further restricted American shipping, as did the resultant war with Great Britain in 1812.

There were natural factors as well, such as the "Great Gale" of September 1815, which wracked havoc on the coastal plantations with unprecedented destruction. Shipowners lost entire fleets, and farmers were reduced to burning dead timber for charcoal and potash to eke out a living. The following year, an unusually cold summer lay frost on the crops numerous times and ruined the anticipated harvest.

Resilient southern New Englanders responded with a surge of small industry, including an increase in the distilling of both brandy from apples and the old staple of rum. But by 1828, with the tariff imposed on the trade, it became cheaper to distill rum on Cuba than Rhode Island.[153]

It was the end of an era for trade and supply between American plantations in the West Indies and farmers and merchants in southern New England. But it was not the end of their ties with supplying southern plantations with slaves, and the growth of manufacturing bound the region even tighter to plantations in southern North America.

3

BROTHERS IN ALMS

The Familial and Economic Ties Between Southern New England and Plantations in the South

Long before the violent political divisions between the northern and southern states of America, planter and merchant families in New England held ties to southern states in both agricultural and business concerns that chiefly generated from ports along the coastline of southern Massachusetts, Rhode Island and Connecticut.

These expansions of northern families to the South came early, according to historian David Hackett Fisher: "A few Virginia farmers were descended from puritan ancestors....the Harrison's, Israel Allenton—son of a London tailor who arrived on the *Mayflower* and resettled in Virginia around 1655 where he married into (Governor) Bailey's Ruling Estate."

By the mid-seventeenth century, a pattern of settlement developed in Virginia: small market villages sprang up along rivers and streams, with small farms and large plantations developed inland. Fisher explained the class separation in Virginia society: "At the top were the Planters who owned much of the land, most of the servants, and nearly all of the slaves in the colony." This "Tidewater Elite," as he termed it, included as much as 10 percent of the adult males in Virginia.

On a visit to the colony in 1724, Hugh Jones noted the customs and habits of the inhabitants of Williamsburg "are much the same as about London, which they esteem their home...they cue in the same manner, dress after the same fashion, and behave themselves exactly as the gentry in London." The description is strikingly similar to that of the Narragansett Planters in Rhode Island. Such similarities between early plantations in southern

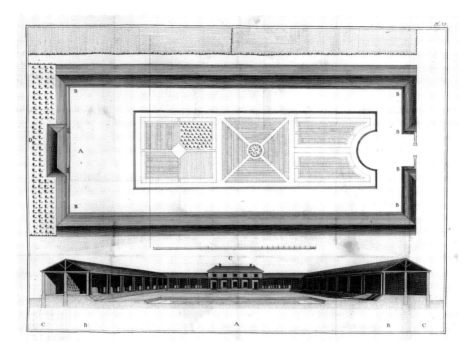

Plan and elevation of a Virginia planter's house, Buisson, Paris, 1791. *Courtesy of the John Carter Brown Library at Brown University.*

New England and those of Virginia, Maryland, South Carolina and other southern colonies included the size of estates and number of slaves, which persisted until the planting of rice in the Carolinas and of cotton in Virginia, Georgia and Maryland.

The North had no such sustainable or profitable crop. Once its forests were largely cleared and the great farms that had sustained herds of cattle and sheep in the hundreds were divided, the northern plantation was no more. While much has been made of the "early emancipation" of slaves in the North leading to the Narragansett Planters' demise, the truth was far more complicated and likely had more to do with great estates carved up by inheritances, leading to dwindling resources and arable land.

A number of those planters and merchants whose families had long supplied the plantations in the West Indies shifted their goods and slaves to the southern colonies. Others had long-standing relationships with merchants or familial ties to southern plantations long before the Revolutionary War. Furthermore, Newport merchants throughout the colonial era supplied the Carolinas with furniture, rum, slaves, horses and a host of other products.[154]

Early Trade with the South

Godfrey Malbone heard good news from merchant Samuel Eveleigh of South Carolina in September 1735: "The season for our rice this last summer has been extraordinarily good, and tho' the bugg formerly mentioned, has done much damage to several plantacons, yet its universally concluded, wee shall make above twenty thousand Bbls, more this year than the last."[155]

The Champlins also ventured to southern ports early. George wrote the following to his brother Christopher from Baltimore:

> *I have dealt here principally with Mr. William Lux a very principall Merchant here who is fond of a voyage to Newport; I have given him some Encouragement that a Cargoe of Flour, Bread, and some Barr Iron, may do there tolerable well in the opening of the Spring, to take N.E. Rum, West India Goods, etc. in return, which will suit him very well.*[156]

Lux wrote to Christopher Champlin himself by way of introduction in March 1766, requesting that Champlin send him a price list of the "Flour, Midlings, Bread Stuff, Bread, Pork, Rum, Sugar, Molasses, Loaf Sugar, Train Oil, and any other articles that you generally send this way."[157] The Champlins also traded for leather goods with John Scott Jr., a merchant in Charleston, South Carolina.

New England produce had a ready market in southern ports. Apples were shipped as far south as Mobile, Alabama.[158] Connecticut and Rhode Island exported bushels of potatoes by the thousands. The Greenwich area of Connecticut produced up to two hundred bushels an acre, while the Rhode Island communities of Smithfield and Johnston were heavy exporters as well. Almost all farms contributed; one family on Point Judith produced from sixteen to twenty thousand bushels yearly, about three hundred bushels per acre.[159]

Howard Russell noted that from "Bristol and Portsmouth Rhode Island; and Wethersfield and South ports of Connecticut, coasters each fall loaded onions by the thousands of barrels as well as hundreds of thousands of ropes to find their market in Boston, New York, and the South."

Historian Paul Coleman noted, "The most successful Rhode Island Merchants had developed a finely attuned sense of locale and timing. Whether they selected their goods locally, or whether they assembled the typical New England Cargo through a series of coastal voyages, they paid scrupulous attention to price, quality, and demand."[160]

S.W. View of the Seat of Henry Marchant in South Kingstown, Rhode Island, anonymous artist. *RHi X17 3019 Courtesy of the Rhode Island Historical Society.*

Aaron Lopez of Newport also traded on a small scale with southern merchants. He traded pipes of wine for rice in North Carolina and received correspondence from Joshua Hart of Charleston, South Carolina, concerning prices there. Hart admitted that his "chief Motive" for writing was to have Lopez place on the "first Vessell for this port…ten hhds of Choice, free from Stillburn and good proof, Jamaica Rum on my own account and risqué."[161]

Rhode Island would also become the northern summer home for many southerners who especially took refuge in "Newport's simplicity and unspoiled beauty. They took long walks on the beach, played lawn bowling, took sponge cake and fresh milk with afternoon tea and danced in the evening. There was an active social calendar printed and reported on in the *Newport Mercury*."[162]

The resort that Newport became known for was largely due to its popularity among Charleston, South Carolina's wealthy families, especially during the "sickly season" down south. "Over 260 families arrived from Charlestown in the eight years leading up to the Revolution, many whose families had made Newport their summer home for generations."[163]

As a likely result of all these factors, Coughtry noted, "After 1750 Rhode Islanders joined English slave traders in furnishing American colonies with Black labor, first in Virginia, and then South Carolina and Georgia."[164]

The Slave Trade with the South

Between 1755 and 1773, trade grew slowly, with Rhode Island sending only nineteen vessels in the trade to Charleston, South Carolina, or Virginia. The disruption of coastal trade by the Revolutionary War depleted even these small figures, but after the war, trade was resurrected in larger numbers due to the ban on trade from America to the West Indies, among other factors.

William and Samuel Vernon, merchants of Newport, are known to have been the first to direct slaves to the southern market rather than the West Indies. As early as 1754, the brothers employed Captain Caleb Godfrey to sail the sloop *Hare* with seventy-eight slaves to Charleston. Subsequent voyages were undertaken by the Vernons, sending Godfrey and the *Hare* back to Charleston the following year with another eighty slaves. This human cargo was traded for barrels of rice for the New England market. The brothers also utilized the brig *Othello* with the southern slave trade, all the while partnering with others and keeping a few ships active in the West Indies.

In 1784 two vessels, the brig *Betsey* and the brig *Gambia* (no owners listed), brought 226 slaves to South Carolina. The following year, the brig *Industry*, captained by the seasoned mariner Benjamin Hicks, transported 150 slaves to Charleston. The *Gambia* also made another journey with 114 slaves, arriving in the port city in July 1786.

The prominent owners of the majority of these vessels used to ship slaves to southern colonies prior to the Revolution were the Vernons and the partnership of Jacob Rivera and Aaron Lopez. Others, such as the aforementioned Benjamin Hicks and Stephen Ayrault, took occasional ventures.

If the letter from Captain David Lindsay written from the African coast in February 1752 is any example, the ship Ayrault and his partner furnished for the venture was in poor shape, and the morale of the captain equally disparaging. In Captain Lindsey's words,

> *I am to let you Know my proceed'gs Since my Last Daited 3th Jan.; and I have Gott on bord 61 Slaves and upward thirty ounces of Goold, and have Gott 13 0r 14 hhd of Rum yet Left on bord, and God noes when I shall Get Cleare of it ye trade is so very Dull it is actually a noof to make a man Creasy my Cheef mate after making foor or five Trips in the boat was taken Sick and Remains very bad yet then I sent Mr. Taylor, and hee got not well and three more of my men has sick. James Dixon is not well now, and wors, then I have wore out my Small Cable, alto oakum, and have ben*

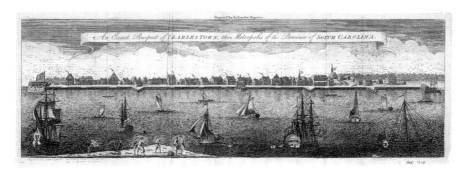

An Exact Prospect of Charlestown, the Metropolis in the Province of South Carolina, London, 1779. *Courtesy of the John Carter Brown Library at Brown University.*

> *oblige to buy one heare…I should be Glad I coold Com Rite home with My slaves, for my vessel will not Last to proceed farr…however I hope She will carry me Safe home once more.*[165]

More common perhaps, during this period, were the individual sales of slaves, or the exchange between northern and southern plantations. Eveleigh's letter to Godfrey Malbone in September 1735, for example, mentioned that in Charleston of late, "There has been imported into this place since the 25th of March last twenty-four hundred negroes, which have sold very well, tho' the greatest part upon credit." It is difficult to tell whether Eveleigh's letter alludes to a market whereby Malbone might purchase slaves for his Portsmouth plantation or the availability of a market for slaves he may wish to ship south.

After the Revolutionary War, fewer of these prominent owners transported slaves to the South but remained fixed on the larger volume they could transport to Havana. For northern planters, the popular appeal of those liberties stated in the Declaration of Independence prompted several port cities, especially in the Carolinas, to ban the import of slaves. The prime slave port in the region then became Savannah, Georgia.

For those larger merchants, trade with the South remained risky. Prices for goods were inconsistent, and ships often lingered in the harbors, trying to dispose of cargo, as evidenced by a letter Captain John Green wrote to Christopher Champlin and Co. from Alexandria, Virginia, on January 4, 1785:

> *I wrote you of the 29th last month informing you of my Arrival at this place, of the dull Sale of our Cargo, of Markets, etc. our Cargo is still on*

board as there is no vent for it at present. Mr. Watson informs me that he has the Quantity of Tobacco already purchased that we shall want to load us, and expects to store the Cargo we have on board as he sees no Prospect of disposing of it. The River last Night froze over which perhaps may be of Advantage to us as there can be no more Supplyes of those Articles whilst the River remains shut up.[166]

That same season, the firm of Burgwin, Jewkes and London wrote to Champlin & Co. from Wilmington, North Carolina, to tell the shipowners, "The difficulty of procuring the Cargo for the *Nancy*, particularly Rice, has hitherto prevented us from making any progress in loading her, but we shall begin in three or four days…tho' it will be near the middle of next Month before we shall compleat what we expect to ship."[167]

A few years later, in 1788, the markets had still not improved. Harry Grant wrote from Charleston on March 14, 1788:

I was in the Country a dunning, when Hulls schooner left this, but to little purpose, since ever I knew this place, people never was so backward in their payments, nor trade at such a stand.…Your Tea remains unsold, and cannot get above 1/8 for it…as to the India Goods nobody would touch them. I tried them at every Vendue in Town. You will see by the Account Sales the horrid Prices they brought.[168]

In one of his last ventures from Cocumscussoc, Gilbert Updike, the son of Lodowick Updike, sailed his schooner *Betsey* to Savannah in 1802, "loaded with cheese, grains, hemp, sugar, and tobacco before continuing on to African coast and from there to the West Indies."[169] The overall reluctance of those established Rhode Island slavers to trade with the South merely opened the door for others, often with little or no experience, to exploit the trade.

The Voyage of the *Dolphin*

Such was the case for shipbuilder and captain Caleb Eddy of Warren, Rhode Island, who undertook what turned out to be a less than profitable venture in 1795–97. He came from a long line of seafaring men, his ancestors buried in the cemetery alongside the Kickemuit River off Serpentine Lane and his own father, Captain Caleb Eddy, lost at sea in

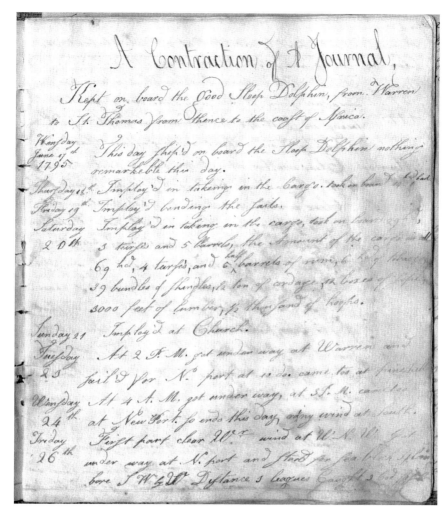

Dolphin ship's log, Warren, Rhode Island. 1795 Ink on paper. Manuscript MSS 828 (Ship's Logs) B12 F2 RHi X17 4269. *Courtesy of the Rhode Island Historical Society.*

1773 and memorialized in the North Burial Ground across the street from his modest house. The son had established himself as a shipbuilder before the Revolutionary War. In the aftermath of the conflict, the economy of the town was almost entirely resurrected by the slave trade.

So it was that Captain Eddy departed Warren in his sloop *Dolphin* on June 21, 1795, sailed to Newport and was then bound "to St. Thomas from Hence to the coast of Africa."

On the twenty-ninth, they noticed a ship standing "Norward and Eastward" whose top mast was "Shod." It was the ship *Sally* from Baltimore, and that afternoon, a boat bearing Captain John Hutchinson was sent over to ask for a supply of water and provisions. Captain Eddy complied, giving them a hogshead of water, fifteen gallons of rum, molasses, a bushel of meat, a bucket of bread and other supplies, for "she was full of famished passengers and short of provisions."

On July 6, the crew believed they had come within five leagues of Bermuda, a mistaken notion as they were actually off the coast of Puerto Rico. The following day, they encountered a brig from Surinam bound for Rhode Island under command of Allen Jacobs. At 8:00 a.m. on July 21, the sloop *Dolphin* arrived at St. Thomas. The crew mailed letters home and went to Blackbeard's Castle while the ship lay at anchor.

For reasons that are not entirely clear, Eddy no longer considered the sloop seaworthy and purchased another. On July 26, all hands were shipped on board the sloop *Rising Sun*. The ship weighed anchor on August 14. Within a few hours, it caught sight of a French ship of eighteen guns but managed to avoid a confrontation. The next day, however, six leagues away from where they had departed, they spied

> *a ship to the westward. She fired 4 shot and we hove too. She stood to the Southard and we sailed away again....*[W]*e saw the ship under our lee. She fired several shots which whistled among our rigging and ordered us to heave too under her lee. He sent his boat on board for Captain Eddy and his papers after examining and searching the chests and vessel and threatening to carry him into Martinique they brought him on board and let us go.*[170]

Light breezes stalled their passage. Some of the crew spied a devilfish but lost half their harpoon trying to haul it in. By the first days of October, they were enduring "fresh gales and thick weather," but forty-nine days out they spied the Canary Islands. The weather cleared, and on October 15, the crew spied turtles in the water, lowered a boat and caught two, as well as a fish, by the end of the day, "which gave us all a fine dinner."

On October 21 at 7:00 a.m., the crew

> *saw the land which we supposed to be the Royal* [?]*, as at 12 we spoke to a boat from Royal* [?] *bound to the Isles Delos....at 2 pm hove out the small boat and Capt. Eddy went onboard the schooner for information at 3 returned, at 4 saw the Isles Delos as we suppose but the weather makes the*

*land appear odd. There being no people on board the schooner but blacks
except one mulatto we liked not there company, at 6 we loaded our guns not
knowing what they might do.*

On November 4, the *Rising Sun* placed twenty-one slaves aboard, along
with some water, and wasted little time clearing the decks and leaving by
five o'clock in the afternoon. They stopped the following day at "Bonnas
Island." On November 12, the crew spent the day "imploy'd in landing the
cargo and ventures."

On Friday, November 20, at 2:00 a.m. the ship's mate noted that "we
had a havy Tornado which caused us to drag our anchor and let go the big
one." The following morning they heard news from the ship *Liberty* "lying at
Surilona belonging to Providence. She had made some trade at Garee, and on
her passage down from thence the slav[s] killed Capt. Potter who commanded
the ship and cut 1 man very bad, but the rest, with killing one slave drove the
rest overboard which was but 6 in number they took the ship again."[171]

The *Rising Sun* put in for repairs, and one "Mr. Cleveland" was sent to find
provisions and slaves along the river Sherborough, with instructions to return
by January, when the ship would set sail again. On December 14, Captain
Eddy boarded a brig from New York, where he heard news of "the sickness
in that Citty which raged to a great height," a reference to an outbreak of
yellow fever that summer. The crew spent Christmas on board with the gift
of a quarter of a goat for their dinner sent from the doctor on land.

By January 14, they were still anchored offshore, and Captain Eddy
boarded a ship from Providence, "Commanded by Captain Sterry who
informed him of some very melancholy deaths," and on the twenty-fourth,
"Capt. Cook arrived here from Rhode Island from which we got information
of Captain Edward Gardner at Garee." The sad news still affected the mate,
who put his thoughts into verse:

> *We in this early youthful age,*
> *Can ease our minds to think of home;*
> *It often makes us for to rage*
> *To think we are oblige[d] to roam.*

On February 18, Captain Eddy took another longboat with four hands to
find Mr. Cleveland along the river Sherborough. Several days later, a Captain
Harris arrived from Warren and brought news of the crews' relations. On
the twenty-fourth, the longboat returned without Captain Eddy.

Sickness then began to spread among the crew and cargo. Two crew members were recorded on March 6 being "very ill" with three days of fever. On Sunday, March 13, Dr. Everson, who had been on the island seven years and expected to set sail as a passenger, died suddenly.

Captain Eddy did not return to the ship until April 9, when the crew learned that he had spent ten to twelve days on a "Bento Island" schooner, where he had lain sick with fever. The captain was better by May, but then the weather turned, and in June, the ship endured another tornado, which caused some damage. On July 7, the mate recorded that "throughout these 24 hours hard gale and raining attended with heavy thunder." The next day, "The wind still continuing to blow a gale with rain and our vessels bottom being so fowl that she will not work to windward and the sea running bad we run under the lee of the Island and lay off on until the tide made against us then we stood to Northward."

On July 11, the crew heard of another uprising on a brig from New York that had left St. Croix and encountered men in three canoes who wanted to trade for rum. Once on board, the men lashed the captain to a gun and heaved him overboard, and then massacred the remaining crew.

Captain Eddy and his crew brought the *Rising Sun* ashore but found it "very much eat[en] by the worms," and a jury on shore ("all the white men on the island") condemned the ship as being "unfit for Sea." The "small"—meaning younger—slaves were placed on shore. Two older slaves brought ashore resisted and were severely whipped. Two crew members went aboard a "Seralon [Sierra Leon] sloop and set out for the island."

The next morning they went onboard the sloop *Fame* and "agreed to work our passage to Boston." The sloop made its way to Bense Island and then to Suralon, where they picked up water and provisions and departed on September 30.

A strong wind kept them leeward of the Cape of Good Hope and prevented them from getting away. By mid-December, the ship had made headway but encountered then "[a]lmost a continual gale of wind from SW to NW which has obliged us to lay too the greatest part of the week." By Christmas, the weather had turned, and they found themselves "not far from Bermudas making the rest of our way to Charlestown." On the evening of January 13, they spied the Charleston lighthouse and weighed anchor. On January 16, the mate recorded that "at 4pm arrived in the town after a passage of 11 weeks from Seraleon off the Coast of Africa."[172]

Eddy delivered the papers of the *Rising Sun* along with 114 slaves to the harbor master and caught a coastal sloop back to Newport. He never again captained a ship to the West Indies, though his son Benjamin Eddy would become a captain and partner for at least three slaving ventures before he turned to whaling. On August 3, 1801, Benjamin Eddy departed Warren in the snow *Eliza*, delivering 114 slaves to Havana, then the prime destination for Rhode Island slavers.[173] In 1806 and 1807, he trafficked slaves to Charlestown aboard his ship *Agent*. The profits from the first voyage and delivery of 139 enslaved to the city allowed him to buy a chosen parcel of land in his hometown, where he would build a large mansion house. His final voyage in 1807 was undertaken without registry at the customhouse or notice in the newspapers, an effort to keep the voyage from the notice of authorities who were prepared to enforce a federal ban on the trade.

The *Agent* traveled to Los, Guinea, as well as drawing 176 slaves from the west coast of Africa before arriving with 157 slaves in Charleston. Eddy's cargo was sold on April 30 at Gadsden's Wharf.

The "Capt. Potter" of whom Eddy wrote in the log was another newcomer to the trade. Abijah Potter was the son of Job Potter, a farmer in Glocester, Rhode Island. He was forty-three years old when twenty-five-year-old Amassa Smith of Newport partnered with him in the slave venture.

Potter sailed the *Liberty* from Providence and reached the African coast but died during the slave uprising mentioned, which occurred between Goree Island and Sierra Leone. Abijah Potter left a wife and three children. Amassa Smith remained in Newport to become one of the most affluent and influential financiers in the city.

In the following years, another seventeen vessels from Bristol, Rhode Island, transported over two thousand slaves to Georgia, many which were financed by the DeWolfs and a veteran slave merchant from Providence, Cyprian Sterry.

Long familiar with the trade to Barbados and Surinam, beginning in 1792 with the ship *Enterprise*, Sterry and his nephew Nathan turned their compass to Savannah. In November 1794, he sent the sloop *General Greene* to the port with 99 slaves. In December, Nathan again captained the *Enterprise* to Savannah, just three months after a slave voyage to Surinam. In 1795, Sterry sent the schooner *James* from Providence and delivered 110 slaves to Savannah. The sloop *Polly*, the schooner *Dolphin*, the ships *Ann* and *Mary*, as well as the brig *Louisa*, all financed by Sterry, departed from Providence to ship slaves to the southern port.

But while Providence had rebounded, other northern port cities like Newport struggled to regain their economic footing. As historian Ellen Crane wrote,

For Newport, independence brought dislocation rather than benefit....[T]he seaport was in shambles, and although the merchants tried to resurrect their failing commercial empire, they were unable to restore it to its pre-war eminence.

Former merchant magnets, such as Christopher Champlin attempted to create a correspondence with shipping houses in Portugal, France, Germany, and Russia, Along with the usual cargo, they began to market tobacco and rice, but the crops from Maryland and South Carolina were scarce, and of poor quality.[174]

Other Champlins partnered with James DeWolf and reentered the slave trade. William Champlin co-owned and captained the brig *Three Sisters* out of Boston, which transported 151 slaves to Charleston in 1805–6. John Champlin also partnered with DeWolf and captained the *Nancy* out of Boston in 1804. Christopher Champlin also ventured into the market again, sending the brig *Fame* to Charleston in 1809.

Bristol remained an active port, with the DeWolf and Christian firm sending out numerous vessels for the slave market in Charleston, delivering most of the 3,900 slaves that ships from Bristol brought into the port

The Ebenezer Cole House, Warren, Rhode Island. *Photo by the author.*

between 1803 and 1807. Warren, during the same period, sent slaving vessels owned by not only Caleb Eddy but also other longtime merchants of the town, including Ebenezer Cole and Samuel and Sylvester Child. These vessels carried approximately 600 slaves primarily from Guinea to the Charleston market.[175]

Many other individuals from southern New England made the choice to come south for an opportunity to strike it rich in a burgeoning market. An early example would be the career of Nathaniel Russell. Born in Bristol, Rhode Island, Russell moved to Charleston, South Carolina, as an agent for a handful of Providence merchants in 1765. Within four years, he had established a shipping firm of his own and, in 1769, launched the ship *Lilly* on a voyage to Africa to procure slaves for the Charleston market.

These were among the most active years of the trade in Charleston, attested by the steady publication of advertisements in the *South Carolina Gazette* announcing the arrival of "prime negroe slaves fresh from the west coast."[176]

In July 1772, Russell wrote to Aaron Lopez in Newport that during the summer there had been "a great many negroes imported here" and there were "many more expected," as the demand let their sale "continue at very great prices." At the age of fifty, Russell married the "wealthy spinster" Sarah Hopton, daughter of a prominent Charleston merchant. By 1795, he was listed as the top merchant in the city, and by 1800, he had built a brick mansion on one of its most prominent thoroughfares. Eighteen slaves attended his Meeting Street home, where he lived with his wife and two daughters.

Nathaniel Russell kept active family and business ties to New England throughout his life. He was the founder and first president of the New England Society of Charleston, a group formed to promote the ideals of Yankee independence and industry and uphold *Mayflower* ancestors as the standard bearers of courage and fortitude.[177]

The reopening of Charleston and other ports in 1804 opened the floodgates, and "slaves poured into Charlestown, primarily on English and Charlestown slavers."[178] Such was the congestion in the harbor that newspapers sounded the alarm about the safety of the water for all the bodies of slaves that could be found along the coastline or floating in the harbor itself.

In the coming decades, the demand for human chattel only grew larger, peaking in the 1830s and 1840s when the pages of southern port city newspapers were filled with advertisements for auctions of "prime" and

"Likely negroes" for sale. While plantation owners often came up from the Deep South to settle affairs and inspect the slaves at market, they left the transportation of those they had purchased in the hands of the factors and drivers in their employ.

Hundreds of thousands of these enslaved people were transported by boat for weeks, malnourished and weakened by the lack of movement during the journey. They now faced an arduous ordeal of being driven along the ancient Indian and buffalo trail known as the Natchez Trace.

Chained or collared together by the drivers, they were "lined up two abreast, with a chain running down the length of the line"[179] and relentlessly driven with the approval of their plantation masters. As historians John Hope Franklin and Loren Schweninger wrote:

> For five hundred miles the trace twisted like a snake through heavy forests, across ridges and valleys, swamps and streams. Some owners and traders thought the journey helped "prepare" slaves for the heat and humidity they would face on the vast cotton and sugar plantations in the Deep South.[180]

Eli Whitney's invention of the cotton gin in 1790 and the resulting widespread production of similar devices expanded the cotton plantations in the South, and demand for slaves to pick cotton grew exponentially. That cotton was, by and large, shipped north to textile mills, especially in southern New England, those mills often run by the descendants of slave-owning planters from the region.

4

A COMMON THREAD

How the Textile Mills Tied New England to the Slave Plantations

Daniel Rodman grew up as a privileged young man and one familiar with plantation living from an early age. He was the great-grandson of John Rodman (died 1698), a wealthy Quaker planter in Barbados. The family had immigrated to Newport with John's son Thomas, who was trained as a physician and came to the North American port city with his fellow Friend William Edmunson.

Thomas Rodman became an eminent obstetrician in Newport, building a fine house on the corner of Thames and Ann (now Truro) Streets. He and his brother John inherited lands in New Jersey and Pennsylvania, and on July 5, 1710, Thomas exchanged five hundred acres of the New Jersey lands for the plantation in Barbados, which had been deeded to his sister. Thomas Rodman also held one thousand acres in Portsmouth that went largely unimproved until his son Clarke inherited the property, built a mansion on part of the land and cultivated the acreage into a farm, where he raised his sons Daniel and Robert.

By this time, the family's interests had expanded to manufacturing. Thomas spent weeks at a time visiting with planters in the southern states. As was common in the era, the sons were groomed for the family business from an early age.

Clarke Rodman's son Daniel (1805–1880) undoubtedly joined his father on a few of these business trips, for by the age of sixteen, he was operating a cotton and woolen mill in South Carolina. On his return in 1835, Daniel purchased a mill in South Kingstown on the Saugatucket

The mill at Mooresfield. *Courtesy of the South County History Center.*

River and turned it into a successful enterprise. Within a dozen years, he had transformed his adopted village of Moorsefield. He built a company store beside the millpond and gave land for the building of a public school. A fine Greek Revival house was also constructed east of the mill and renovated through the successive years of prosperity that continued through the Civil War.

The success of the Rodman Mill allowed him to purchase the Barber Mills some seven miles away at Glen Rock in 1866, and he constructed a new mill of Westerly granite. His oldest son, Daniel Brown Rodman Jr. (1837–1896), would oversee the new venture.

Daniel Rodman Sr.'s younger brother Robert Rodman (1818–1903) inherited the large estate from his father and managed the farm much as it had been during the plantation era. He expanded the family's interests and began his own manufacturing of "kersey" and "Kentucky jeans," clothing made of a course woolen-cotton blend, specifically to be worn by slaves.

Samuel Rodman (1800–1882) purchased a series of small mills at Rocky Brook, off the Pawcatuck River just north of Peacedale, Rhode Island, and promptly constructed a single woolen mill to manufacture woolens and jeans for the southern market. The company-run Rocky Brook store would

Portrait of Robert Rodman from *Representative Men and Old Families of Rhode Island. Courtesy of the South County History Center.*

be overseen by Samuel's son Isaac, who by 1860 was advertising dry goods and textiles for sale in the *Narragansett Times*.

The Rodmans, however, were one of the few Newport families that attempted a transition from maritime ventures to manufacturing. The majority of those early efforts came from the descendants of the Narragansett Planter families.

Eli Whitney's patent of the cotton gin in 1794 was the tool needed for this economic expansion. The inventor's letter of that year to Thomas Jefferson explained that his contraption would significantly increase the production of cleaned cotton as "one negroe [could] clean fifty weight," or fifty pounds of cotton per day. Within fifteen years of Whitney's patent, the South was supplying more than half of Great Britain's demand for cotton and also supplying the growing textile mills in the North. By the 1830s, northern mills consumed over one hundred million pounds of slave-picked cotton for manufacturing.

Rhode Island contributed to the rise of manufacturing early on, having established tool and die works in Providence by the close of the eighteenth century. The state was prepared more than others to meet the demand for machine parts related to the textile industry.

As Cole noted in his book *The Transformation of Rhode Island*,

> *The ability to design and build improved equipment, the high quality of workmanship, and the central New England location gave Rhode Island textile machinery firms the capacity to capitalize on the opportunity created by the rapid expansion of cotton and woolen manufacturing....By the 1820's they operated as small but full fledged enterprises and formed a major though highly specialized segment of the base metal industry.*[181]

By far, the greatest contribution made to the ties southern New England families held with the southern plantations was through the cotton mills that grew along nearly every river, stream and pond in the region.

A statement written by J.K. Pitman, agent of the Providence Manufacturing Company, in 1809, gave a prospective investor an early picture of the burgeoning industry:

> *There are in this state sixteen Cotton Mills in operation and seven more erected which have not yet begun to open…also within thirty miles of this town, there are ten at work & six not yet in operation.…The Mills within the state contain between 13 & 14,000 Spindles, and consume about 12,000 lbs of cotton weekly. Those without contain upwards of 6,000 spindles & consume about 5,000 lbs of cotton in the same time.*[182]

Pitman described the hand "picking" of cotton, as well as the loom work to make the yarn, performed by "private families, & wrought by females during the hours unoccupied by their domestic concerns." He estimated that his branch of the firm employed more than four hundred families during a considerable portion of the year, as well as "many around the mills, who have an indirect agency in the production of the business." The first among those to invest in the new industry were the descendants of those planters who had supplied goods and slave labor in the Atlantic for over a century.

As Christy Pejura-Clark detailed in her scholarly volume *Dark Work*, early ventures into manufacturing in South County strengthened the ties with slavery: "Once dependent on slave labor, the Narragansett Country became increasingly dependent on slave-grown cotton and the southern slave clothing market."[183] Contemporaries and sometimes partners with the Rodman family, the Hazard family developed a manufacturing enterprise with northern and southern roots that expanded up to the outbreak of the Civil War.

The Hazard Family

The patriarch of the Rhode Island family, Thomas Hazard Sr. (1720–1798), ran a large farm in South Kingstown. "College Tom," as he was called (he was the first in his family to be formally educated), became a devout Quaker and an early abolitionist in the state. His eldest son, Rowland, however, felt differently. In 1789, Rowland moved to Charleston, South Carolina, to partner with his cousin John Robinson Jr. and establish the firm of Hazard, Robinson & Company.

In Charleston, the firm had a growing reputation solidified by Rowland Hazard's friendship with the Charleston commission merchant Isaac Peace and subsequent marriage to Peace's daughter Mary. Hazard ventured in his own commission firm with Peter Ayrault in 1796 but dissolved the firm in 1803. He inherited the Rhode Island farm after his father's death in 1798 and moved back to the state by 1802, when he invested in the small textile mill that Benjamin Rodman had built on the Saugatucket River. During the same period, he and brother Thomas Hazard Jr., who had established a merchant house in New Bedford, Massachusetts, invested in coastal trading, including the importation of cotton from southern ports.

Rowland Hazard improved the mill in South County, introducing a carding machine and power loom before turning the business over to his sons Isaac Peace Hazard (1798–1879) and Rowland G. Hazard (1801–1888). The brothers bought out all other investors by 1826, and the firm became a family operation, renamed **R.G. Hazard & Co.** The youngest Hazard, Joseph Peace Hazard (1807–1892), was admitted to the firm two years later.

While the mill had once relied on local wool and cotton for manufacturing, under the brothers' expansion, the mill became more dependent on cotton imported from the South. The mill began shipping back its woolen goods and premade clothing to plantation owners in Alabama, Mississippi and Louisiana. Their development of custom-made clothing catering to individual owners' demands shifted orders away from Great Britain to the entrepreneurs of New England.

I.P. Hazard spent much of the 1820s and 1830s as a traveling salesman, visiting southern plantations whose slave populations ensured that robust orders would continue to flow back to the company in Peace Dale. On March 7, 1835, he wrote from West Baton Rouge, "I have agreed with Wm. Garso Johnson of this parish to send him immediately 400 yds double kersey, 400 yds single D.K. at 40. Single at 35. payable in January next. He wants them sent immediately and directed to be put on board one of the regular packet steamers at New Orleans."[184]

He wrote of the vigor's of travel from Baton Rouge:

[A]s *I was at the point of leaving N.O. I came to the plantation which Cousin Jacob has charge of, I rode a horse from there to this place about 80 miles & 120 from New Orleans or 150 by land….*

I have been 4 days riding here stopping at most of the principal plantations on the way. I think there is a great opening here for the double Kerseys made stout.…Some of the planters will want the thick all wool at

The Hazard Mill in Peacedale, Rhode Island. *Courtesy of the South County History Center.*

53. The double kerseys they will buy at 40. and it will be very important to give them an article which will weather well.

An invoice for "two hundred yards of your double kersey" was shortly after received from L.T. Hobson & Co. of New Orleans.

I.P. Hazard wrote to his brother again from New Orleans later that month after arriving from "my excursion to Baton Rouge, having been absent about 12 days & visited abt. 300 plantations—I have made engagement which will scatter our cloths among the planters very generously—They almost all want the double kersey and think it an excellent article."[185] Looking toward the future, he wrote that the building of an iron forge was in the works along the Mississippi River, though he advised that it was prudent for them to move slowly but deliberately, as the southern planters were "not yet ready" for the technology already working in the Northeast.

Rowland G. Hazard also traveled to the South, making yearly visits during the winter months of the decade between 1833 and 1843. The observations of slavery he made during his travels for the firm changed his mind on the justification of slave labor. He provided legal assistance to free men of color who had been falsely seized in New Orleans as runaway slaves. The mill he ran in Peace Dale employed free Black laborers for carding and spinning.[186] By mid-century, the company had grown at such a fast pace that the firm employed agents in major southern cities to expedite business. Plantation owners used these agents as well.

These "factors," as they were called, were an integral part of the "long chain of middlemen linking plantation owner and manufacturer, who through his contacts, helped the isolated, rural planters earn the best price in the volatile world-market."[187]

Factors were commonly from New England and served more than the purpose of a broker or agent. They purchased a planter's supplies and often advised on financial matters; in general factors knew the state of a plantation far better than the owner. Likewise, they knew the market better than the Rhode Island and Connecticut merchants whose ships plied the waters with needed goods. Factors could inform owners of a glutted or depressed market and apprise them of what goods were bringing better prices. Often these factors were family members of invested southern New Englanders. When Christopher Champlin wrote to Savannah seeking advice on current markets he wrote to Joseph Wanton, a member of a prominent Rhode Island family that had relations in Barbados, Newport and Savannah as part of their family enterprise.

648
ISAAC PEACE HAZARD.

651
ROWLAND GIBSON HAZARD.

Left: Portrait of I.P. Hazard from *Representative Men and Old Families of Rhode Island. Courtesy of the South County History Center.*

Right: Portrait of Rowland G. Hazard from *Representative Men and Old Families of Rhode Island. Courtesy of the South County History Center.*

Among the planter families who invested in cotton manufacturing was Daniel E. Updike, cousin of the last owner of the family plantation in North Kingstown. The venture was apparently unsuccessful, for in May 1813, he wrote to William Ellery from Wickford:

Honored & Dear Sir,

On my return from Providence last week I received your letter....

I propose to go to Providence again tomorrow or next day in order to see to my Cotton [mill?] *as well as other businesses. There are a number of Persons who want to purchase, but those who have the money want to obtain at a very reduced price and I am not willing to sacrifice too much Capital to carry on the mill & could be in Providence to see to the business—I have no doubt that I could clear $5000 dollars per year by it after paying all charges.*[188]

An old mill at Biscuit City Pond in North Kingstown was purchased in the early nineteenth century by twenty-six investors who formed the Narragansett Cotton Company. The company president was James Helme Jr., a storekeeper in Little Rest, with others on its board of directors, including William Peckham, a farmer and appointed judge; Cyrus French, a hatter; John T. Nichols, a saddlemaker; and deputy sheriff Elisha R. Gardner.

The company acquired a $2,000 loan from the Narragansett Bank and constructed a large three-story building that measured thirty feet wide and sixty feet long. Many of its workers were housed in smaller structures nearby, though many of the local women and children were laborers in the mill. Millworkers began their day at 5:00 a.m., with a stop for breakfast at 6:00, and then resumed work until noon, when it was time for lunch. Afternoon work continued until 6:00 p.m., when supper was allowed, then work again continued until the day ended at 8:00 p.m. When it grew dark, everyone labored under the dim light of tallow candles.[189]

The Davis Family

The Davis family of North Kingston began with Joshua and Mary (Scott) Davis, the first settlers of what would become Davisville, the site of a gristmill constructed by Joshua Davis. His two sons, Jeffrey Davis (1780–1854) and Ezra Davis (1779–1863), continued the mill and also partnered in establishing one of the first woolen mills in Rhode Island. Before 1820, their mill was carding and finishing wool produced from their own and other local farms. It was woven by the local cottage industry. By 1824, the brothers had partnered in the manufacturing firm of E&J Davis, producers of "negroe plain," the cotton cloth for slaves that would later be called "Kentucky jeans." Davis's account book shows the growing dependency local laborers came to have on the firm. Locals provided carpentry work, repaired roads, built bridges, cleaned out the dye house trench and supplied other general labor.[190] His correspondence reveals the difficulty in collecting debts from both local and long-distance clientele.

An associate wrote to the Davises of these matters in July 1839:

> *I was very much disappointed in Mr. Wilber, however I think we may yet get the whole by holding on to our demand until he can compromise with most of his creditors, he owed so little and being a young man. I think if*

we do in that way we shall get our demand, his Father is a man of some considerable property I have been told, if that is the case it makes our chance still better.…Your particular friend (J.B. Ames) has arrived from the South, he can't attend to any business at present he expects to start for the [?] in the course of a week or two, when he returns he will be ready to attend to business but not before. I inquired of his Lordship whether he had collected anything of Mr. Arnold as yet, he has not nor is he likely to from what I could learn from his conversation.[191]

Jeffrey's son William Dean Davis joined the firm in 1835. He also entered into the wool business for a short time with his relations James Brown Mason Potter and Elisha R. Potter Sr. under the firm Davis & Potter. He left the family business and purchased his own mill in Centerdale by 1852 and went on to own the Uxbridge Woolen Mill. William Dean was also the prime stockholder in the Quidneck Manufacturing Company.

The son of Elisha R. Potter expanded his father's enterprise when he inherited land at South Ferry and Usquequag village. Just two years after Elisha Jr.'s inheritance in 1837, he constructed Independence Mill, so named because it was raised on the Fourth of July. With the opening of the mill, Potter Jr. became the youngest mill owner in Rhode Island at the age of twenty-one. The manufacture of "Kentucky Jean Cloth" for the clothing of the enslaved was profitable enough that Potter opened a second mill at South Ferry.[192]

The Arnolds of East Greenwich

Colonel William Arnold (1739–1816), Revolutionary War militia leader and owner of the tavern Bunch of Grapes, where the Kentish Guard formed, became the patriarch of a large and extended Rhode Island family. The son of John Arnold, he married Alice Wilcox on May 2, 1765, and they raised nine children. His son Stephen, born later that year, joined his father's mercantile firm, and the partnership of William Arnold & Son engaged in trade with ports in the Caribbean, as well as Surinam and French Guiana. They obtained goods from local suppliers such as William and Stephen Greene, Caleb Coddington, Clark Brown, Joseph Howland, Holden Rhodes and George Mumford, sending the sloop *Providence* with "Sundres" on numerous trips to the West Indies during the 1790s. By the turn of the century, the firm peddled goods with merchants in New York, especially Greene & Lovet.

Stephen Arnold wrote to the firm, "Gent, We expect in the space of ten or 11 days a cargoe of molasses of the first Quality; will you plan to inform us, what price in your opinion, it will bring."[193]

They also speculated in land holdings in Ohio. The family also kept active in local interests, owning two fishing vessels: the schooner *Roby* and sloop *Polly*. They ventured in the coastal trade, especially after entering the textile manufacturing business.

Another son, Perry Greene Arnold (1772–1819), spent much of his life serving as captain and master of trading vessels owned by William Arnold & Son.[194] His travels often took him to a southern port, on to the Caribbean and back south again. Perry Greene Arnold was master of the brig *Betsey* for a venture to Alexandria, Virginia, in 1806.

Leaving East Greenwich in late June, the crew experienced fair sailing until the afternoon of June 26, when squally weather, accompanied by "Sharp Lightening," hit. The next few days brought heavy gales, and they were not again under full sail until the thirtieth. The next five days brought a return of pleasant weather with mild to variable winds, allowing the crew time to mend the battered sails. On July 5, the crew greeted the brig *Diana* under "Capt. Morris, 13 days from Porstmouth for Simarer [Sumeria?]."

Gales and heavy rain returned the following day. They encountered the ship *Hazard*, out from Halifax, Nova Scotia, on the fourteenth day of its voyage. They steered west, hoping to escape the gale "and let us proceed on our course," though "moderate gales" continued. By July 9, they were enveloped in "smokey thick weather," and "all hands [were] imployed in braking out the hole in order to trim the ship." The latter part of the day brought calm winds, and the next dawned calm, with a "hot Scalding Sun." The ship limped along through more "moderate gales" until it reached Barbados on the afternoon of July 20. The next morning, the crew landed the deck load of horses, sixteen bushels of corn, and hay.

In 1807, the firm wrote to Charles Cadogan of Barbados, that "we received…H.M. Cavans draft on Wm Wood, Baltimore, for one thousand dollars. The firm transported goods also to merchants Greene & Lovet in New York.

The Arnolds of Providence

Richard James Arnold Sr. (1796–1873), son of Welcome Arnold, a Providence patriot and early abolitionist, was destined to follow his brother Samuel into the family shipping business or perhaps choose to enter the flourishing textile manufacturing trade with his brother-in-law Zachariah Allen. Instead, he married Louisa Caroline Gindrat in 1824, and when Louisa inherited White Hall, a large plantation in Bryant County, Georgia, the couple thereafter divided the year seasonally between the plantation and the Arnold home in Providence as well as a summer home in Newport.

Arnold spent considerable time accumulating land in the South during the years leading up to the Civil War. Near the end of a lengthy, detailed letter to his attorney concerning his record of lots purchased in 1836, he mentioned,

> *Mr. Blake died the Tuesday last very suddenly of apoplexy—the Saturday previous I* [hailed] *him on the road going to Savannah.—Had he much property in his own name with you or was it in McLaughlin's name?…If in his own name & a sale should be effected…a company might be formed to buy & no doubt would get the property very low, some of it* [seems] *to be very valuable.*[195]

In 1857, his account book shows that he held 11,000 acres, the land and buildings on it worth an estimated $100,000. His livestock included 200 head of cattle, 150 sheep, 12 horses and 11 mules. The slaves on his plantations numbered "200 people young & old @ $450.00 per head."[196]

He had invested heavily in the production of cotton at White Hall and at Cherry Hill, bringing innovative scientific methods to the plantations and also tracts of land along the Ogeechee River, which made him the most prosperous rice planter in the region.[197]

As Arnold's biographers wrote:

> *Richard Arnold valued his plantation site on the Ogeechee River southwest of Savannah for its accessibility to the Savannah market, the river functioning as a highway to bring in supplies and to ship out the cotton and rice. But even more important…the Ogeechee was a tidal river, essential to the tide-flow method of rice culture by which the flow and ebb of the tides were used to flood and drain the fields.*[198]

White Hall Plantation, Bryant County, Georgia. *Photo by Greg Lowry, courtesy of White Hall Plantation.*

To improve this method, Arnold devised a "system of dikes, ditches, and floodgates, more elaborate than any used by textile manufacturers for their mills." Though Arnold was absent from his plantations for five months of the year, he was considered a working planter and kept detailed information on the efficiency of planting, tending and harvesting the crops.

In late February, the first rice fields were ready for planting. Detailed instructions left for an overseer in 1842 attest to the tedious labor slaves underwent from planting to harvest, not least of which was dictated to those who were elderly or too young to perform the daily labor required. These slaves were called "bird minders" by the planters, and their sole job was to stand in the wet rice fields and drive away the migratory birds that could strip the rice fields of the sprouting crop.[199]

In the first week of March, the corn fields—Arnold grew forty acres at Cherry Hill for market—were bedded, as were potato fields prepared with fertilizer, and the cotton fields at White Hall were ploughed as well. Work on the rice and cotton fields continued all week, as did the planting of the corn, most of the field hands being thus occupied. Others mended fences or any breaks in the dams of the floodgate system.

Three weeks after the firing on Fort Sumter, Arnold sold the plantation in Georgia to his son Thomas Clay Arnold and removed his family once

G.N. Jones Newport stables of his "Cottage" called Kingscote (1839) on Newport's Bellevue Avenue. *Photo by the author.*

again to their Newport home. Both of his sons remained in Georgia, overseeing the family concerns. Richard Arnold's brother-in-law Zachariah Allen also flourished in trade.

In addition to the extensive family, a small group of paternal and close friends in the Arnolds' circle were neighbors in Newport as well. George Noble Jones and his wife, Mary Nuttall Jones, often invited the Arnolds to spend time in their Savannah home. G.N. Jones was born in Georgia in

1811 to Noble Wimberly and Sarah (Fenwick) Jones, both of whose families held a lengthy colonial heritage. G.N. Jones came to manage the family plantation owned by his mother and aunts in Jefferson County. In 1839, he hired architect Richard Upjohn of England to design Kingscote, his summer cottage on Bellevue Avenue in Newport.

The following year, he married the widow Nuttall and by marriage inherited the El Destino and Chemonie Plantations. El Destino was established with the purchase of some 7,638 acres of government land by John Nuttall, a wealthy planter from Virginia and North Carolina. His son William purchased the property from his father's estate in 1832. His widow, Mary, inherited this plantation and purchased Chemonie Plantation, just six miles north of El Destino, from Hector Braden, a family friend.

George Noble Jones inherited his family plantation as well, and the couple were content to socialize in Newport during the summer and spend the winter in Savannah with its mirror of fine homes and social calendar. Unlike Arnold, G.N. Jones seldom visited his plantations, preferring to correspond with his overseers and rarely interfered with their management of the land and slaves.

Henry Augustus and Harriot Kinloch Middleton bought a stone cottage just north of the Joneses' summer home. The Middletons owned Weehaw Plantation in Georgetown, South Carolina, Harriot having inherited the 1,818-acre estate on the Black River from her father in 1823. The Middletons continued to successfully grow rice on the plantation, which held a total of 302 slaves in 1850.[200]

The Arnold Family of Warwick

On February 12, 1813, Warwick entrepreneur James Utter Arnold determined to establish a cotton mill and signed an agreement with widow Abigail Francis securing rights to "clear and dig and straighten and sink not lower than tide water a certain brook leading from the Warwick road at a place called JENKES WADING place into the cove or Salt water sufficient for the purpose of conveniently letting all the water from the wheel or wheels which may be erected at the brook."[201]

Francis was the daughter of merchant John Brown of Providence, and the brook from which Arnold, and others—including Thomas L. Greene, Thomas Stafford and Amos Lockwood—secured their riparian rights to the waterway, flowed through a large meadow on the seven-hundred-acre Occupasstuxet

Farm. Arnold was the son of Captain George Arnold, who had captained a vessel in the merchant trade, running chiefly to the West Indies.

In 1814, James Arnold entered into agreements with John Waterman & Son and housewright John W. Arnold to construct a dam and pond at the brook and to raise a mill or "such other buildings as will accommodate them."

The mill was erected on land that had been purchased by Zebulon Utter in 1765. Arnold named the mill the Utter Manufacturing Company. It was completed in 1814 and operated 12 power looms and 550 spindles. Local markets were obtained for the mills shirting production, and the following year, brother George C. Arnold was dispatched onboard the ship *Telegraph* to Charleston, South Carolina. While George drummed up business in the southern markets, James Arnold continued to oversee the mill in Warwick, which by 1832 employed five men, six women and eleven children. By 1834, according to the *Niles Weekly Register*, the company held 1,900 spindles.

The mill continued to produce cotton goods until about 1838, when it was destroyed by fire. The business, however, was carried on for many years by James Arnold's eldest son, William Utter Arnold.[202]

Zachariah Allen of Providence

Zachariah Allen was born into a prominent family, educated at Phillips Exeter Academy in New Hampshire and groomed for a career in law. He graduated from Brown University in 1813, set up practice and in 1817 married Eliza Harriet Arnold.

Law proved an unsatisfactory career, and Allen soon became interested in the textile industry. In 1822, he invested in a woolens factory. Allen established the Allendale Mills and the Georgiaville Mills, utilizing his factories as experimental laboratories for his refined power looms and cloth finishing machines. He invented high-speed shafting with loose belts and developed a cutoff valve for steam engines. Allen also worked at constructing fireproof areas of the factory and founded an insurance firm.

He was close to brother-in-law Richard J. Arnold, helping him with the purchase of a steam engine to modernize his rice plantation at Cherry Hill. He oversaw Arnold's northern estate, serving as trustee while the family was in Georgia. The family house in Providence—the former Sabin Tavern of great celebrity from the days preceding the Revolutionary War—was modified and moved from its original location, often rented for the winter.

Allen collected the rent for the house and oversaw maintenance on the mansion house.

When the Civil War erupted, Allen disclosed in his diary that he would consider it a blessing if the free states should separate from the slave, as "all history demonstrated that the existence of slavery has first corrupted and then destroyed every republic in which it has been admitted." Allen's own family was deeply divided—his nephew Thomas owned slaves and, with brother William Elliot Arnold, joined the Confederate army. Two other nephews, Crawford Allen and Tristam Burges, along with grandson Andrew Robeson III joined the Union cause.

Allen never quite discerned, despite those diary-inscribed proclamations, that his support of Arnold's plantations made him complicit with slavery. Allen was active in many charitable and civic organizations in Providence, but his own obsession with increasing his mills' profit margin blinded him to the humanity hidden behind the machines.

The Lippits of Providence

The Lippit brothers, Charles and Christopher, began their textile venture in 1809 while Charles was a merchant in Providence. That year, the brothers invested with Benjamin Aborn, George Jackson and Amasa and William Mason in organizing a cotton mill named the Lippit Manufacturing Company.[203]

Charles Lippit served as a factor for the firm in Savannah. His son Warren (1786–1850) took to the sea at sixteen and was commissioned a captain by the age of twenty-two. He sailed the ship *Factor* from Providence to Savannah in October 1810, writing his "Remarks for Savannah river": "Steer in from Sea West by Compass & when you make the Light keep it bearing West-when within 1½ miles of the light steer W. b. N. & anchor abreast of the light within ½ mile of the shore."[204]

Warren Lippit spent nearly a quarter century at sea before returning to join the family textile business. He married Elizabeth Seamans in 1811 and moved to Savannah to partner in dealing with groceries and cotton.[205] In 1818, he purchased one lot of land in the New Leeds section of Savannah, from one John Lillibridge, presumably for a house, but he traveled often between his adopted city and Providence.

His son Henry Lippit was born in Savannah but would be educated at the Kingston Academy in Rhode Island. On graduation, Henry worked

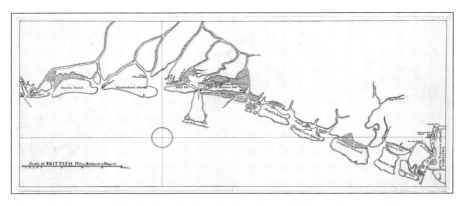

Chart of the Florida and Georgia Coastline from St. John's River in Florida to Savannah, 1740. Courtesy of the John Carter Brown Library at Brown University.

four years as a clerk in the firm of Burr & Smith in Warren. He moved to Providence in 1835 and took a job as a bookkeeper with Josiah Chapin & Co., one of the largest cotton merchants in the city. By 1838, he had partnered with Edward Walcott and Amory Chapin in the commission business. The firm dealt principally in bale cotton and print cloths.[206]

In 1848, Henry with his younger brother Robert L. Lippit, also born in Savannah, purchased, along with other Providence capitalists, the Tiffany Mill at Danielson, Connecticut, from owner Comfort Tiffany of New York. The property held three hundred acres, extensive undeveloped waterpower and a mill, which held a capacity of three thousand spindles. The following year, a new mill with a capacity of ten thousand spindles was built, and the company reformed under name of the Quinebaug Manufacturing Company. With the death of their father in 1850, new partners Amos and Moses Lockwood bought a controlling interest in the company. The brothers then hired the Coddington Mills to continue their cotton manufacturing. In 1854, they sold their shares in the Quinebaug Company and invested in the Harrison Mills, located in Woonsocket.

On Robert's death in 1858, Henry purchased his share in the company, which by 1860, on the verge of the Civil War, held a capacity of forty thousand spindles. As with factors, local manufacturers employed commission merchants to ship their goods back south from Rhode Island and Connecticut.

William Perry Greene, a descendant of Revolutionary War hero Nathanael Greene, was part of the partnership begun in 1815 with his first cousin Franklin and another relation named Samuel. The firm of F. & S.W.

Greene conducted business up and down the Eastern Seaboard, using ports at East Greenwich and Providence as well as New York. The family forge on land and fleet of sloops in the water all contributed to the nation's cause in the Revolution. Now the ships, schooners and sloops employed by the cousins shipped trousers for slaves in Rio de Janeiro, as many as 7,700 pairs of "napkins" (trousers) in one voyage.

Greene married Mary Olney, furthering his connections among Rhode Island's merchant families. The cousins shipped goods from the family mill of the Potowomut Manufacturing Company, as well as other local textile manufacturers such as the Hope Manufacturing Company, the Kent Manufacturing Company, and the Union Dye Company and the Georgia Cotton Manufacturing Company. They also brought Jamaica rum, muscovado sugar and molasses to the ports of Savannah, Charleston, Norfolk and Alexandria.[207]

William Perry Greene wrote numerous letters in regard to accounts with various business firms, including Otis Dunlop & Co. slave auctioneers in Richmond, Virginia. In a letter dated November 1, 1818, Greene wrote regarding an "invoice & bill of Lading for two cases Cotton Goods for the sloop *Phebe*, the present serves to advise of my having drawn on you for four hundred dollars in favour."[208]

He likewise advised local mills on shipping and, as the market often had fluctuation, asked them to keep him appraised of market value for their goods. In a letter to Charles Potter & Co., founder of the Natick Mills, Greene wrote, "I have on board the *Mount Hope* to your address three cases of Cotton Goods one of ticks & two of shirting which I wish to dispose of immediately on their arrival.…[O]blige me by frequent advices of the state of the market for all description of cotton goods and the progress you make in the Sales of the Cotton Threads."[209]

Such evidence shows that the shift to textile manufacturing and the continued ties of southern New England merchant families to the South expanded during the first half of the nineteenth century and actually progressed up until the time of the Civil War.

In 1845, seventeen of the forty Rhode Island textile manufacturers listed in *Niles Register* specialized in cloth for slave garments. At the time, this was more than any state and more production than all the southern states combined. The 1860 census of manufacturers still listed Rhode Island first in production of mixed cotton and wool "satinets, linseys, kerseys, jeans, and negro cloth."[210]

Massachusetts investors also fed the industry, mills sprouting along nearly every waterway in the early years of the nineteenth century. Among the most notable, and those who would be powerful opponents of the antislavery movement, were a group called the "Boston Associates," which included Francis Cabot Lowell, his brother-in-law Patrick Tracey Jackson, Nathan Appleton and Abbot Lawrence. These men founded the Boston Manufacturing Company in 1813 and opened their first mill along a stretch of the Charles River in Waltham a year later. The Waltham mill was the first in the United States to use a power loom. The success of this mill led to other endeavors by the associates, including the purchase of the Pawtucket Falls waterpower, site of the Slater Mill, and establishing the Merrimac Manufacturing Company in 1821, around which the mill village of Lowell would be established.

The Boston Associates also introduced what would become known in the textile industry as the "Waltham-Lowell" system, considered more humane than the employment of children as within the British industry, and carried on in the Slater Mill of Pawtucket. The mills in Waltham and those later established in Lowell, Massachusetts, employed young women between fifteen and thirty-five years of age to operate both looms and other machinery for mass production of high-quality cloth. Employment came with opportunities for advancement and education. The women were also paid in cash at the close of the week. Such benefits offered incentive to many "mill girls" during the early years of industrialization.

At their height, the mills at Lowell were employing some eight thousand women and men, and the high-production spindles and looms were turning the nearly two million pounds of southern cotton imported each year into fifty-eight million yards of cloth.[211] The founders of the Boston Manufacturing Company purchased southern cotton and utilized the advances in technology, a motivated workforce and the power of New England's rivers to "make cloth as good as, and cheaper than, British imports."[212]

The economic downturn of the 1830s, however, and the resulting cut in wages resulted in the organization of a "Factory Girls" union. The women staged a pair of unsuccessful strikes in 1834 and 1836 but would become more fully organized in 1845 with the formation of the Female Labor Reform Association.

Several members of the Boston Associates became active in politics. Nathan Appleton served in the General Court of Massachusetts through several terms between 1816 and 1827 and was elected to Congress, where he served from 1831 to 1833 and again in 1842 in the House of Representatives. His political endeavors earned him the nickname of the "Cotton Whig," as he secured tariffs on foreign import of textiles to give the American industry every advantage.

As the abolitionist cause grew in fervor, Appleton found himself at odds with both friends and family. Charles Sumner, a longtime family friend and visitor to the family's "cottage" in the Berkshires, would soon draw him into the political fray after becoming a member of the Senate. Appleton's daughter Fanny married the poet Henry Wadsworth Longfellow. As a pair, they supported Sumner and the abolitionists, the late-evening discussions held in their Cambridge home seemingly miles away from the attitudes of Appleton and his neighbors on Beacon Hill.[213]

Abbot Lawrence

Ten miles downriver from the Appleton mills on the Merrimac River, Abbot Lawrence and his brother began their own enterprise in 1814 as importers of goods from Britain and China. The firm of A.&A. Lawrence soon included interests in textile manufacturing and the Suffolk Bank, a clearinghouse on State Street in Boston.

In 1830, the distressed mills of Lowell, Massachusetts, prompted the firm to restructure and reopen the mills as the Suffolk, Lawrence and Tremont companies. The brothers also owned the power rights to the stretch of river than ran through what would become the town bearing their namesake. From 1845 to 1847, a village and two mills, the Atlantic Cotton Mill and Pacific Cotton Mill were established along the Merrimac.

As with Nathan Appleton, the manufacturer engaged in politics, as a fellow Whig and ardent protectionist. Abbot Lawrence would ultimately achieve more prominence during his career. Elected to the Twenty-Fourth and Twenty-Sixth Congresses, Lawrence was considered for placement as the vice-presidential candidate on the ticket with Zachary Taylor in 1848. After a diplomatic posting in Great Britain, he returned to his family's business in 1852, separating himself from the party due to his disenchantment with their stand on the issue of slavery.

The Whitins

Mills proliferated as well along the Blackstone River, a tributary of some seventeen miles from Blackstone, Massachusetts, to Pawtucket, Rhode

Island, where Samuel Slater had placed his early mill at Pawtucket Falls, where the Blackstone became the Seekonk River. Among those who established mills early along the river was Paul Whitin. Originally from Dedham, Massachusetts, Whitin came to Northbridge after the Revolutionary War and served as an apprentice to Paul Fletcher, an iron forger in town. In subsequent years, Whitin married Fletcher's daughter, and the two men established the Northbridge Cotton Manufacturing Company in 1809. Built on the west side of the Mumford River, a tributary of the Blackstone, the original mill was a two-and-a-half-story wooden-framed building that held two hundred spindles. At the time, it was only the third mill established in the Blackstone Valley. In 1815, the pair, along with Fletcher's sons, established the Whitin and Fletcher Cotton Mill. This lay on the opposite side of the Mumford River and held some three hundred spindles. In 1826, Whitin purchased the Fletchers' interest and built the brick mill that began the large complex of Paul Whitin and Sons, later to be named the Whitinville Mill.

The success of the mill allowed them to expand in 1830 and again in 1845, eventually employing some 145 townspeople. His four sons—Paul Whitin Jr., John C. Whitin, Charles Pickney Whitin and James Fletcher Whitin—continued to grow the family business, buying up failing mills during the economic downturn of the 1830s. Their textile expire would eventually include mills in Linwood, Riverdale, Rockdale and Uxbridge, Massachusetts.

By 1860, New England held 52 percent of the cotton manufacturing concerns in the country and operated 75 percent of all spindles and looms in operation, Massachusetts and Rhode Island accounting for 30 percent and 18 percent, respectively, of that number. The mills consumed 283.7 million pounds of cotton per year, or 67 percent of all cotton purchased by United States manufacturers.[214]

Southern Competition

Mills in the American South also competed for the slave cloth market. Historian Madelyne Shaw documented the growth of the industry in Columbus, Georgia, dating from 1844 and the opening of the Coweta Manufacturing Company. At its onset, the mill produced mainly spun yarns and osnaburg, a rough cotton fabric originally made from flax that was used for curtains, upholstery covers and fishing wear. The Coweta Manufacturing Company also produced a small line of rope, thread and linsey, which was made into shawls and winter dresses. The mill preferred to hire poor white women and girls, who worked in family groups.[215]

The Mississippi Manufacturing Company was selling cotton thread locally when in 1850 the mill installed looms for osnaburgs and linseys along with carding machinery. By the outbreak of the Civil War, the company was in full production of yarns, jeans, linsey and kersey. Another Mississippi firm was the Woodville Manufacturing Company, which opened in 1851. The Woodville Company competed directly with the mills of Lowell, Massachusetts, by producing its own brand of "Lowell bolt," a plain cotton used for sheeting, shirting and other domestic uses. "Woodville Cotton for Negroe Clothing and Cotton Sacking" was advertised to compete for southern dollars. In 1852, the owner dismissed the last of his white workers and ran the mill fully with slave labor to decrease his expenses to the bare minimum.

As secessionist fervor grew, more southern planters looked to these manufacturers, but they proved small competition, having neither the machinery nor the financial backing to outpace the mills in southern New England.

Ultimately, northern mill owners would find a resurgence of industry in the South. By the close of the nineteenth century, many owners had abandoned their old and outdated mills in New England to reestablish their business in the cotton belt. Local leaders wooed the New Englanders by "emphasizing the region's advantages of abundant land, cheaper labor, energy sources, lower taxes and transportation. Promotors also promised New England investors with company towns free of union influences and restrictive laws concerning the health and safety of industrial workers."[216] Many workers migrated south with the mills, giving the northern states a shortage of labor for those mills that did remain.

5

NEW ENGLANDERS IN THE SOUTH

In the fall of 1784, Revolutionary War general Nathanael Greene was, among others, on the trail of merchant John Banks of Virginia. Banks and his firm of Hunter, Banks & Co. had been the sole merchant to apply for the position of supplying the southern army during the campaign. As commander, Greene had agreed to deal with Banks and passed along drafts for clothing and supplies authorized by Robert Morris, the nation's superintendent of finance. Greene had authorized drafts on his own personal funds, believing that Banks would honor his advance payment to the men for clothing.

When Charleston merchants balked at taking the drafts in payment, Banks crafted a scheme, luring two American majors in collusion to use the military mail for correspondence and payments. Under Banks's direction, those drafts from the government were used to buy tobacco in Virginia, where "growers would accept the drafts in exchange for the tobacco—a real, durable good. The tobacco would then be shipped to British Islands in the West Indies, where cash from its sale would be given to the merchants that had sold clothing to Banks."[217]

The result of this scheme was that Banks traded with the enemy, entrapping two American officers with charges of treason. Additionally, Banks never paid the merchants but ferreted the funds into other schemes. By the spring of 1784, he had run out of credit, and soon after, Greene was hearing rumors in letters from friends and, worse, from creditors in London.

Greene did not know of the extent of the situation until he arrived at Charleston during a sweltering heat wave in August 1784. Creditors came knocking at his door almost immediately after his arrival, and he found that he was accountable for some $30,000. To make matters worse, Greene learned that Banks had come by one of his plantations in South Carolina and, professing that he had cleared his debts to the overseer, procured yet more money, fleeing the scene for parts unknown.

When the weather cooled in September, Greene undertook the hunt for Banks. He eventually tracked him to the small town of Washington, North Carolina, arriving on October 1, only to find that Banks had been killed and buried two days before. Greene was desperate to clear his debts and return to Rhode Island, where his wife and children waited in a rented Newport home.

He borrowed a horse and rode on to Richmond, hoping to settle matters through his attorney, but left for home facing the grim reality that his only hope in avoiding debtors' prison lay with those plantations and slaves given him by the Carolinas and Georgia in appreciation of his military service. Greene had accepted these gifts of plantations confiscated from exiled Tories in 1783, receiving some 6,600 acres in South Carolina along the Edisto River and the more promising Mulberry Grove plantation in Georgia, which already contained "a very elegant house" and some 1,300 acres, much of which was valuable swampland for cultivating rice.

Greene, one of the premier officers of the Continental army, had supported the enlistment of slaves to earn their freedom in the army. His cousin Christopher Greene was named commander of the First Rhode Island Regiment, which became known as the "Black Regiment" and consisted mostly, at its inception, of slaves who were permitted to enlist for service. He had notably petitioned the legislature of South Carolina to create a similar regiment to assist him in the southern campaign.

But with the war's close, he faced incredible debt and ruin. He therefore viewed these ventures of managing plantations the same as his investments in privateering, and his Basto Iron furnace in New Jersey, both of which failed to turn a profit. Nonetheless, that spring, he procured more slaves for his South Carolina plantation, and hired carpenters to spruce up the house at Mulberry Grove. Greene moved his family to another house as well, uphill from the dank wharves, which he hoped would improve the fragile health of his five children and his expectant wife, Catharine (Caty) Littlefield Greene.

His wife gave birth to their sixth child in August while Greene was in New York, once again trying to settle his debts. When he arrived home just

The majestic equestrian statue of General Nathanael Greene, sculpted by Henry Kirke Brown at Stanton Park NE, Washington, D.C. *Photograph by Carol Highsmith, Library of Congress.*

a few days after the birth, he found that the children had all come down with whooping cough, and the baby, christened Catharine, died within the month.[218] The bill for the child's coffin came just a few days after the funeral, and Greene grumbled that the whole town anticipated their departure, and as such, "those people knowing I am going away harass me to death for a number of little debts."

In mid-October, Greene, Caty and their five children—along with their tutor, the Yale-educated Phineas Miller—sailed for Charleston, South Carolina. For the man who had but two years before written "I feel for Rhode Island what I cannot for any other spot on earth," it was the last he would glimpse of his beloved state's shore.

On arrival at Mulberry Grove, they found the estate still very much in disrepair, with many windows in the upstairs of the house, the bird coops and greenhouses shattered. To worsen their woes, before their arrival, a slave who had been sent out with the cattle lit a fire to shoo birds from the rice crop; it burned out of control and razed the entire field.

Greene also learned that a ship tied at the dock in Savannah had sunk with forty-five barrels of rice from the plantation. The former general wrote in near despair to Henry Knox, "My family is in distress and I am overwhelmed with difficulties and God knows where or when they will end. I work hard and live poor but I fear all this will not extricate me."[219]

Greene's premonition came true. That spring, E. John Collet, the agent for the London firm to which Greene was indebted, arrived in Charleston, and he soon began receiving letters for a hearing. Greene answered with a litany in which he plainly laid out his hardships but ultimately agreed to a meeting.

Negotiations began in May 1786, and the men agreed to meet again on June 12 to finalize a payment plan. Greene surely felt relieved, and within that month, a settlement was reached with the estate of John Banks, yielding Greene even more real estate. With the settlement, he owned the entirety of Cumberland Island, the eighteen-mile-long sea island off the coast of Florida. Greene even mused about moving his family there to escape the heat and miasma of the low country.

Greene met with Collet again in June and concluded a schedule for payments until the debt was ended. That night, he and his wife, Caty, strolled the plantation owned by John Pendleton, a former aide-de-camp during the southern campaign in the Revolutionary War. He fell ill that evening, a condition that included excruciating eye pain and an alarming swelling of the forehead, for which he was bled. The former second-in-command of the Continental troops died within the week.

With the general's death, that might have been the final, unfortunate chapter in the family's ownership of a southern slave plantation—certainly it is implied in several biographies that Catharine Greene had every intention of returning to Rhode Island. Several of her late husband's friends, including Brigadier General Anthony Wayne, who was master of the adjoining plantation, and Phineas Miller, the tutor who would successfully manage the plantation, dissuaded her from selling the property.

Nathanael Greene had placed much of his real estate as security against his debts, and after Caty sailed to Newport that summer and met with attorneys and creditors, it became clear that it would take years to settle the estate and her family would be obliged to return to Mulberry Grove and live off the proceeds of the plantation.

Within a year, the plantation, under Miller's supervision, was flourishing, despite Caty Greene's letters depicting her woes during her travels of the household belongings being carted off by creditors. She petitioned Congress for the money that Greene had paid Charleston merchants for his troops' clothing, writing in part, "Can Congress…be deaf to the Miseries of the widow and fatherless—No—I will not yet believe mankind so ungrateful, so unjust—I ask no favors but Justice."[220]

Despite the wording of her letter to Congress, the widow Greene managed the affairs of her former husband adroitly over the coming years, receiving support from such luminaries as Washington and Lafayette, while liaisons and luncheons with advisors and creditors staved off any serious threat to the plantation and other lands she was determined to hold. In 1790, the plantation received a visit from President Washington during his southern tour of the states. In 1791, Caty Greene's petition was approved by Congress, and she was awarded $47,000.

The following year, a young man by the name of Eli Whitney from Connecticut arrived as a prospective tutor on the plantation. He was an acquaintance of Phineas Miller, who had recommended him for the job. The position never materialized, but Whitney was encouraged to stay, Mrs. Greene being greatly impressed with his mechanical abilities. She also advised him to study law under the guide of her own attorney Nat Pendleton. He preferred to tinker on the plantation and wrote to his father:

> *During this time I heard much said of the extreme difficulty of ginning Cotton, that is, separating it from its seeds. There were a number of respectable men at Mrs. Greene's who all agreed that if a machine could be invented which could clean the cotton with expedition, it would be a great thing both to the Country and to the inventor. I involuntarily happened to be thinking on the Subject, and struck out a plan of a Machine in mind.*[221]

Whitney showed the plan to Miller, and they soon formed a partnership in the firm of Miller and Whitney, with Caty Greene's backing. An upstairs room of the plantation house was converted into a makeshift laboratory in which a crude model was constructed. Within months, Whitney completed a full-scale model powered by one man and a horse that could clean an amount of cotton that would have taken the labor of fifty slaves. By the spring of 1793, Eli Whitney's cotton gin was in full production at Mulberry Grove.

In time, Catharine Greene secured a live oak contract with the government on Cumberland Island. She invested much of her fortune in the production of the cotton gin, as well as in a land development plan promoted by a group of New England industrialists, including son-in-law John Nightingale, called the Yazoo Company.

The company's plan, put forward in 1795, was to purchase some thirty-five million acres from the state of Georgia extending as far west as the Yazoo River, a tributary of the Mississippi. Their offer of $500,000, a fraction of its worth, was nonetheless accepted by the Georgia legislature. But before the check could be signed, a storm of protest erupted, and the sale became a scandal. It was learned that Georgia legislators in both the House and Senate were given free shares in exchange for votes; the "Great Yazoo Fraud," as it was coined, collapsed.

Eli Whitney had opposed any investment in the industrialists' plan, and a rift soon developed between the partners. Several New England friends who had moved South in expectation of making their fortunes returned home. The failure of the scheme cost Greene and Miller their ready cash, tied up their estate property pledged for collateral and severely compromised the cotton gin firm.[222]

Pirating of Whitney's invention had begun, and Georgia farmers, now suspect of Miller and Whitney, by association, gained ground in their efforts to have the company's patent rights set aside. Miller and Whitney fought back with a patent suit that was heard in a Savannah courthouse in May 1797, after which the jury ruled against them. The partnership was dissolved, and Whitney signed a contract with the federal government to manufacture firearms. Catharine Greene Miller was forced to place Mulberry Grove on the market with an advertisement in a Savannah newspaper. No buyers came forward, and the estate eventually went on the auction block.

In 1800, the Millers moved to where Catharine's daughter Patricia Greene Nightingale and her husband, John Nightingale, had built a home on Cumberland Island, lands that were part of the settlement with the estate of the man Nathanael Greene had once chased south.

A New Englander Visits a Southern Plantation

As indicated in the previous chapter, as the nineteenth century progressed, more New England industrialists were seeking to mete out the middlemen in their production. If a northern mill family had the wealth to purchase a plantation in one of the southern states, their profits increased. If extended family members transported the cotton north and the finished cloth south, a small empire grew in the trade. One of these families was the Arnolds of Providence, portrayed briefly in the preceding chapter. The journal of Arnold's sister Eliza Arnold Allen provides a glimpse into the lives of these "transplanted Yankees."

In April 1837, Eliza Arnold Allen visited her brother Richard J. Arnold's plantation in Georgia. She arrived at Cherry Hill after a series of steamboat journeys along the southern coast. Eliza spent much of the time socializing with family and visitors to the plantation, but she was also a spiritual woman, devoting time to visit among the slaves and share readings from the Bible she carried with her to the slave quarters.

On April 17, she wrote,

> *Richard and myself set off about ten for the Clays—It was quite warm—but an hour after we arrived we went to visit all the homes on the plantation & saw the Negroes who were at home. I had a present of thirteen eggs from some of them which as I could not offend, I accepted to carry home—and today brought some pieces of cake…in return.*[223]

Eliza seemed to share her brother Richard's belief that slaves could be educated and Christianized and become happier slaves for the effort. She admired the efforts of the school on the plantation in producing "wonderful black scholars" and praised the efforts the schoolmistresses had taken in "tracking down the negroe hymns" with which they entertained Mrs. Allen, as well as "those they learned themselves." Some had "delightful voices," and "she and her sister sang well themselves."

This was apparently a favorite exhibition of the women, for the next day, the Black students were called again to serenade another visitor, for "she would leave on the morn and had never heard the negroes sing." Eliza continued her visits on the grounds of the plantation, writing, "One can see them all as they are in the fields in the morning…and towards evening they are at work for themselves." Among the rows of small houses, she found "an excellent old woman and as I explained to her the pages of the Bible I felt that I could learn much more from her than I could impart. She is humble contented and cheerful—and constantly [?] upon her heavenly father for every helping—I feel that she has many—At her house were several of the negroes of this place & two from Col. McAllister's."[224]

Eliza Arnold Allen sympathized with the lot of a planter's wife. She recorded,

The wife of a planter as much as the planter himself is placed in a very responsible situation—so many souls committed to their care. Many think it an easy situation but it is from ignorance that they form such an opinion. No one who has not seen, can imagine the constant calls upon their time and patience. No day passes that the attention is not called to someone sick, & to many wants which are always freely made known.

Mrs. Allen's journal betrays the tension that began creeping into transplanted New Englanders' consciences around this period over what to do with their slaves. It was a tension her brother Richard attempted to overcome by his example as a "progressive" planter, one who educated slaves and treated them in what was thought of then as a favorable manner.

This northern example transplanted to the South did little to impress their neighboring planters, nor did it carry much weight with their New England friends and acquaintances. During those decades that Richard Allen was "improving" the lot of his slaves, free Black people in northeastern states were organizing clubs for the improvement of Black men, public lectures and conferences, culminating in the National Convention of Colored Citizens, held in Buffalo, New York, in August 1843. Black orators such as Frederick Douglas, Henry Highland Garnet and William Stills drew large crowds of enthusiastic listeners. Stills, along with Harriet Tubman, had much to do with working with white abolitionists, including William Lloyd Garrison and Quaker leaders Thomas Garret and Levi Coffin to conduct the Underground Railroad, the collection of routes that secreted away as many as 500,000 slaves to freedom by 1850. The abolitionist fervor that was growing in the region soon took embodiment in Massachusetts senator Charles Sumner.

Sumner's early career was in the law, his mentor at Harvard Law School being Supreme Court justice Joseph Story. A man of many interests, Sumner traveled throughout Europe to broaden his education, and when he returned to Boston in 1848, he had decided upon an active role in the struggle.

His first act was to openly criticize sitting congressman Robert C. Winthrop—descendant of the colonial governor—for his stance on the annexation of Texas, as well as his support for the war with Mexico. Both were endeavors that the administration clearly hoped would expand territory and, by extension, soothe those neighboring slave states by allowing the new states themselves to determine whether slaves would be among their population.

Sumner took part in protest with fellow "Conscience Whigs" against the party's nomination of slaveholder Zachary Taylor for the presidential ticket and supported former president Martin Van Buren. On June 28, 1848, before a large audience in Worcester, Massachusetts, Sumner condemned the complacency of Congress, decades after northern states voted for emancipation, in stonewalling further measures to curb the trade and catering to southern states that threatened succession if Taylor did not win.

He also took aim at the industry that supported the ongoing trade more than any other form of commerce with the New England states, calling out those "lords of the lash, and lords of the loom" for the ongoing collusion between the mill owners and southern planters. In the din of the noisy campaign that year, Sumner likely felt that his words had little effect. While they likely received little notice in Washington, the movement was having an effect on the mill owners in New England.

In 1850, Rowland G. Hazard gave an impassioned antislavery speech before the Rhode Island House of Representatives, indicating his regret and revulsion toward those who profit from slavery. When the mill that had produced kersey burned to the ground in 1855, the Hazard brothers ceased production of "negroe cloth."

This was also the year, however, that Congress revisited the long-ignored Fugitive Slave Law that had first been enacted in 1793. Now, the body once again complaisant to the wishes of southern states (lest they secede) gave the new law more teeth and the power to enforce the return of slaves to their masters. The passage of the law outraged northern abolitionists and became one of the key elements of the storm that led to war.

It is little wonder that Richard J. Arnold built a summer home in Newport, where a small enclave of southern elite remained. The Balls, Izards, Jones, Middleton and Nuttall families all brought their slaves with them for the season. The Arnolds' lives in Rhode Island differed little from the South but for the climate.

Such ongoing business interests made northern mill owners not only complicit with the ongoing institution of slavery but also compatriots with those who supported the Confederacy and fought to keep the nation and its people divided. As war became eminent between North and South, many of these southern elite "walked a tightrope between the appearance of support for the union cause and the reality of their southern sympathies."[225]

A longtime summer resident, "Old Mrs. Pickney," voiced her support loudly for the Union, which only led to suspicions on the part of her neighbors, who knew that her two grandsons had joined the Confederacy. When she returned South in 1862, she confided to a friend that she was "very happy…to be back on southern soil."

6

RECONSTRUCTION AND THE DECLINE OF THE PLANTATIONS

The decline of the plantation economy was a slow and torturous process for those enslaved and a source of frustration for those who opposed slavery. The end of the American Civil War hardly meant the end of the southern plantation or the cotton trade from which the plantations had grown. And if the northern victory brought together the nation as a whole, it was hardly a unified country, nor were the northern industrialists free from promulgating those continued divisions as the politics suited them. President Andrew Johnson promoted a reconstruction program that some felt was too soft on the southerners. Other radical members of the Republican Party moved, with some success, to reshape southern society itself by transplanting northern farmers and manufacturers to rural counties and educators to instruct Black children.

While the postwar South struggled to renew its agricultural economy, the owners of the large plantations found themselves with a continual shortage of labor. Many freed Black women attempted to withdraw from the hard toil of field labor and devote more time to their children—now free to be educated rather than exploited. Male laborers could now come and go as they chose, no longer obligated to work for one master, or to be disciplined by a cruel overseer. Many would fight to become landowners themselves as compensation for their years of slave labor.

As Eric Foner, the foremost historian of the era, noted, "The Planter class…had no intention of presiding over their own dissolution. It wanted railroads, factories, and northern investment so long as those supplemented and invigorated the plantations and did not threaten the stability of the black labor force."[226]

Traditionally, the plantation economy had worked against any economic enterprise that would threaten the labor force. The same was true of those southern plantations that had held whole counties throughout the Carolinas, Georgia and Tennessee in the grip of economic dependency on the planter establishment.

Forward-thinking newspapers might extol the virtues of breaking up the plantations "into respectable farms" and of bringing cotton manufacturing to the South for the benefit of "our young men" who "must learn to work," but as Foner pointed out, this vision of economic change never had the majority support among southerners.

Moreover, the wealthy northern merchants favored Johnson's reconstruction purely to help along the revival of cotton production—still the reunified nation's leading export. Without such a revival, northern merchants believed, southern plantation owners would default on their debts, and as a result, New England's textile mills would be forced to close—the nation itself would lose sufficient specie and fall short of paying its own foreign debt. Senator William Sprague of Rhode Island, whose own family loomed large in the industry, and thus in state politics, warned that New England would become "bankrupt in every particular."

Economic change came painstakingly slow. Between 1868 and 1872, some three thousand miles of railway expansion crept into southern states, but railroad companies faced increasing construction and operating costs. By 1872, many were on the verge of bankruptcy.[227] Port cities such as Charleston and Savannah, which had once hosted the ships that transported slaves and cotton, now languished with near-empty harbors. Other ports that the railroad bypassed suffered the same fate.

While white southern politicians demanded that cotton continue to be produced by Black labor, white farmers began making inroads into the market, especially where the railroad had extended its reach. The development of cotton cultivation in upcountry counties in South Carolina, Georgia and Alabama as well as the newly developed farms in Texas, Arkansas and Louisiana shifted the geographical location of commercial cotton farming. Conversely, the cotton cultivated by Black laborers by 1876 fell a full 30 percent from the crop sixteen years earlier.

The hoped-for revival of the industry was fraught with difficulties—most of the white yeomen who invested in the agricultural revival were already burdened by debt from the war. Crop failures, increased taxes and, by the

1870s, a precipitous decline in agricultural prices all contributed to the plan's failure.

Those upcountry plantations, around which whole communities gathered, found themselves increasingly indebted to merchants, who often provided the only source of credit in regions with few banks and less capital. As land values plummeted, merchants advanced loans only in exchange for a lien on the year's cotton crop. The policy forced indebted farmers to concentrate on their cotton crop, thus further expanding production and depressing prices.[228] Under these pressures, tenancy for poor white yeomen and sharecropping for Black freedmen became the primary forms of labor in the South.

Most historians have stated that sharecropping came about through concession to freedmen's demands for proprietorship of land. Looking back, it can hardly be debated that plantation owners had no intention of deeding land to former slaves. Sharecropping scattered Black families and undermined efforts by Black mothers to spend more time with their families and educate their children.

As each family's economy now depended on the output they produced, women and children were often compelled to return to field labor. A description of their day-by-day existence shows how difficult it would have been for any life away from toiling in the fields: "In southern Louisiana the harvest season for the two great crops, cotton and corn, ended only a few weeks before planting began again: ploughing, planting, picking cotton, gathering the corn, and pulling out and burning stalks took up the whole of the four seasons of the year."[229]

Laborers cultivated cotton much in the same way as corn, planting a single stalk in hills spaced roughly two feet apart, followed by months of repetitive hoeing of the weeds and grass. When hoeing was finished, they donned a bib-like pocket garment hung about the neck that extended nearly to the ground. With these, "walking and stooping up and down the rows, they pulled the ripe cotton bolls off the branches and filled their sacks."[230]

It was difficult work, and to earn the most money, these former slaves were up before dawn and picked cotton until it was "too dark to see." They sometimes continued working the fields by the light of the moon. Planters on the larger estates encouraged competition among the laborers and often promised the workers "a great feast" after the harvest had been gathered.

While plantation owners railed against the loss of control over their labor force and resented the new sharecropping economy, they soon established "country stores" on the former plantations while other white merchants did the

Postcard of Houmas House, Louisiana. *Author's collection.*

same at crossroads of the communities grown up around the sharecroppers' plots. The resulting indebtedness ensured that no sharecropper families could save money to purchase the land they worked, and tenant farmers also grew less likely to overcome their debt.

When economic recovery did come, Black farmers shared in the relative prosperity that came with high cotton prices at a time of increased production. Former slaves were still unable to obtain land, but Republican newspapers trumpeted the increased wages, the rising number of depositors in the Freedman's Bank, the increase in rentals of land by Black tenants and the actual money they now had to spend in the stores.[231]

Between 1872 and 1877, cotton prices declined sharply, dragging the value of tobacco, rice and southern-manufactured sugar down as well. The resultant ripple effect through the planter economy forced many farmers into poverty and diminished the little resources of credit they had. As Foner wrote, "Many planters who had weathered the postwar years saw declining land prices sharply reduce the value of their holdings, while falling agricultural earnings made it impossible for them to discharge their debts to local merchants at the end of the year."[232]

Congress's effort to aid the South through credit capsized in 1873 with the bankruptcy of Jay Cooke & Co., one of the leading lenders to southern loan holders. The resulting depression of 1873 turned efforts away from

economic development in the region. Many farm owners defaulted, and wages plummeted as the rate of unemployed workers rose exponentially.

By 1875, over 150 of the planters who owned estates in the once wealthy Natchez region of Louisiana had lost part, if not the entirety, of their property due to unpaid taxes or other debts. Small planters initially lost their land to larger estates, but with time, the control of Louisiana's sugar plantations would lie in outside hands.

The Decline of the Plantations

For those among the Newport enclave, none fared worse than George Noble Jones, whose Georgia plantation lay straight in the path of Union general George Sherman's devastating and infamous "march" to victory. The Union troops all but destroyed the plantation house and outbuildings and burned a crop of some five hundred bales of cotton valued at more than $100,000. While his Florida plantations remained active and productive, the estate of El Destino would no longer be the family's home.

Richard J. Arnold and his wife, Louisa, returned to White Hall after the war and set about repairing and redecorating the mansion. The sons who had overseen the plantations during the war were, by 1870, taking steps at furthering their roots in the South. Thomas, who still managed the lands of White Hall, was engaged to Elizabeth Screven, daughter of a wealthy Savannah financier, and his brother Eliot was courting her cousin.

No matter how earnest the Arnolds' efforts to reconstruct their prewar lifestyle, the reality proved to be far different. Their small circle of loyal domestic servants likely kept up a pretense of old times within the household, but in December 1865, the Black workers on the plantation, now freedmen, chose to voice their mistrust of Thomas Arnold and refused to sign a labor agreement. They would not leave the plantation and resisted any attempt to forcibly remove them from the land. The former slaves who had long worked on the plantation were threatened by an influx of new freedmen that Arnold had persuaded to work there. Signing a fair contract that would secure their labor was paramount to their interests, in that it set each worker on an equal footing, and those former enslaved workers would not be treated in the future as de facto slaves.

The Black laborers stood their ground until a satisfactory contract was negotiated through the Freedmen's Bureau. The Bureau's representative, one Captain Cook of Rhode Island, made subsequent visits to the Arnolds at White Hall and held meetings with Black workers at Strathy Hall on the nearby MacAllistar plantation. The Arnolds' plantation ledger shows that their payroll for the planting season of May and June 1867 was $1,700 and that the total expenses for the planting seasons between 1866 and 1868 were more than $60,000.[233]

Louisa Arnold died in Newport, Rhode Island, on October 15, 1871, in exile from her beloved White Hall. Richard J. Arnold spent one more winter on the plantation before returning home to Providence, where he died on March 12, 1873.

On Richard J. Arnold's death, his son Eliot acquired the lands at Cherry Hill plantation. He built a new house for his wife in 1874 but was not a successful manager as his father and brother had been. The plantation was ultimately put up for public auction to settle his debts.

Thomas Arnold inherited White Hall with its mansion house. He continued to manage the plantation as he had since the outbreak of the Civil War. He held plans for great expansion at the time of his father's death, having purchased the nearby Cheves rice plantation in 1872. Such hopes for expansion would not come to fruition. He succumbed to illness on December 23, 1875.

On Thomas's death, the estate was broken up, and White Hall was sold at public auction in 1877, though the Arnolds' still managed to hold a connection to the plantation. The winning bidder was George Appleton, the wealthy husband of Richard J. Arnold's granddaughter Lulu. The couple returned to the mansion, and Appleton promptly turned the estate into a retreat and hunting lodge for his circle of gentlemen friends.

The Fall of Oak Lawn Plantation

Another of these southern elite whom the war stranded in Newport was Mary Walton Porter, who by the outbreak of the conflict had long been a summer resident of the city, returning each winter to Oak Lawn, the plantation she had inherited in southern Louisiana. In the 1860 census, she held 407 slaves.

Mrs. Porter was originally from Nashville and married James Porter, the second son of his namesake, a famous minister and activist in Ireland. His sons Alexander and James would both excel in law and become prominent

Photograph of Oak
Lawn Plantation,
Louisiana, by Bill
Fitzpatrick. *Courtesy of
Wikimedia Commons.*

members of the Louisiana bar, Alexander ultimately becoming a Supreme
Court justice and James serving as attorney general. James Porter inherited
the plantation from his older brother in 1844 and promptly moved his family
from a smaller plantation he owned in West Baton Rouge Parish.

His widow seems to have managed the plantation with the assistance of
the merchant commissioners Leverich & Co. The New Orleans firm, like
many other merchant commissioners, often effectively ran plantations in the
owners' absence. Leverich & Co. exported such products as rice, tobacco,
hemp, hides and bulk chemical products such as saltpeter. As cotton factors,
they arranged the shipment and sale of the crop of Louisiana planters.
Since the early nineteenth century, the company was one of the prime
shippers of sugar, molasses and rum.

Mary Walton Porter and her two daughters Annie and Mary remained
in Newport during the war. The conflict had considerable effect on the
southern economy, and both the Porters and the firm suffered from the
loss of trade and ready cash. Upon the conclusion of the conflict, the firm
made a rapid recovery and leveraged control of the property, holding the
mortgage to the plantation. In 1873, after the death of Mary Walton, the

firm purchased Oak Lawn plantation, as well as a smaller neighboring estate named Dogberry that was also owned by the Porters. The sisters were allowed to remain in the mansion house until such time as the property was sold.

Leverich & Co. went into liquidation just six years later, and the Porters seem to have regained title to the property. One of the firm's owners, however, seemed to have been lured by the charm of the old plantation. Edward Leverich took steps to purchase Oak Lawn in his wife Annie's name and, through negotiation, secured the property from the Porters in 1881. It was to be theirs and the plantation's ruin.

Much of the initial monies to revive the plantation were taken on credit provided by his cousin Abe Leverich, also a commission merchant in New Orleans. As the estate had fallen into disrepair, new machinery, farm implements, livestock and even barbed wire for new fencing had to be procured. Just as these improvements were underway, the plantation's levee broke, flooding most of the arable land. The same occurred a year later in 1883. Bad weather ruined crops, and the machinery in the sugarhouse broke down. Leverich's debt grew deeper, and he borrowed money from both his father, Henry S. Leverich, and his father-in-law, Frederick Schuchardt. By 1885, he secured a contract with the Burdon Central Sugar Refining Company, which would build a refining plant close to Oak Lawn and have exclusive rights to the plantation's crop for the next three years.

When Edward Leverich died in November 1886, his wife, Annie, assumed control of the property, and in the following year, she breached the contract her husband had reached with Burdon Central and allowed another company to refine the sugar in 1887 and 1888. The resulting lawsuit, despite her attempt to countersue, left Annie Leverich unable to maintain the plantation. By December 1887, she had determined to sell the plantation and in March 1888 found a buyer in Colonel R.E. Rivers, the proprietor of St. Charles Hotel in New Orleans and an investor in a number of old estates as far afield as Tennessee.

Rivers revived these estates as retreats for the genteel families who remained after the war. On these old plantations, surrounded by the luxuries of the past—and no doubt served by Black domestics—southern families could relive the past before that "recent unpleasantness" perpetrated by the northern zeal for abolition.

By the early twentieth century, the plantation was again in disrepair. In 1927, it was purchased by Captain, C.A. Barbour, a former steamboat captain who had often passed within sight of the plantation while navigating the Teche River. Barbour had made a fortune in the Texas oil fields and invested heavily in reconstructing the house, but before plans were completed, the house was ravaged by fire, leaving only the columns and the brick walls remaining. Undaunted, Barbour rebuilt the house, and his re-creation remains today.

LONG BURIED AND FORGOTTEN

Finding the Traces of Slavery in New England

O n the opening page of Rhode Island blacksmith "Nailer Tom" Hazard's diary, which "Began June the 21ˢᵗ 1778," he recorded a typical voyage of a flag, or transport vessel, that hauled off that morning from "Tom Robinsons whaf" and anchored off Fort Point that night. The next morning, they set sail again and arrived off Warwick Point around sunset.

A Black man, free or enslaved, we do not know, had died on board the vessel. A party rowed out from the ship toward the shore. Nailer Tom recorded the event in what would be the Quaker's customary terse, matter-of-fact manner: "George Coggishall,[234] Negro man died on Board, we Buried him on the beach, the Son was in the clips."[235]

This small incident recorded during the colonial era is one of but many circumstances in which Black individuals, considered mere property, were buried in innumerable, now anonymous places of New England. While the quick burial on a beach was the fate of many slaves who died conveniently near an island or peninsula, those who arrived and labored on plantations were buried in designated plots on the property or in larger designated areas known only to locals as the "slave burial ground" or "old Indian burial ground," as existing indigenous grave sites were also incorporated for use as slave burial grounds.

In later public cemeteries, the lots where slaves were buried expanded into the "potter plots" of the nineteenth and twentieth centuries. As lands were sold within urban areas, both family and slave plots within cities were dug up and the remains and gravestones moved into the public cemeteries. There, slaves were further separated from white burial grounds or, in some cases, forgotten completely.

As Rhode Island was foremost in the population of slaves per capita during the colonial period, our focus will be mostly on those known sites of burial in the state and those still hidden among the remaining woods and suburban sprawl, as well as those now lost to history.

Some enslaved or freedmen like George Coggeshall have only a name recorded in a diary or a ledger book to speak of their existence. Others have nothing more than perhaps a lot number, or the recording of a stone at some time in an overgrown plot. Certainly the largest graveyard holding the bodies of the enslaved is the Atlantic Ocean. Rhode Island slavers played a large role in committing dead, dying and sometimes rebellious slaves to the watery deep.

By 1760, Rhode Island vied with North Carolina as one of the busiest slave trading colonies in the world. According to statistics compiled by the archivist of the Little Compton Historical Society, Captain Nathaniel Briggs alone, working first for Newport merchant Aaron Lopez and then independently, was responsible for "the forced transport of 2,166 enslaved people and the deaths of 267 people during their middle passages from Africa to their points of sale."[236]

By Jay Coughtry's table of Rhode Island slaving voyages, looking at a period during the triangle trade from 1751 through October 1775 alone, Rhode Island vessels lost some 653 slaves on these voyages. Those lost in the later trade with the southern states number in the thousands.

On land, the height of the trade also meant the peak of plantation activity, and the greatest population of slaves resided on Narragansett plantations in South County. In many cases, former field hands or domestic slaves continued to work on the farms where they had lived and had been raised after manumission.

When they died, they were buried in the same lots with others who had never gained their freedom. Even if they had left the plantation and earned a living on their own, if their estate did not provide a burial plot, they often were often consigned to the burial ground on the plantation where they had been held captive.

Daniel Updike, one such plantation owner, penned a sardonic comment in his daybook with the return of a particularly troublesome slave, who now had to labor for fish, clothing and shoes, "*Sic Volvere Parcas*," a quote from Virgil that may be translated as "so turns fate," reflecting the misfortune that many former slaves encountered in having little recourse but to work for their former masters.[237]

Still, author Glenn A. Knoblock in his *African American Historic Burial Grounds and Gravesites of New England* noted that

New England slave owners seem to have given the enslaved some measure of latitude and freedom in their burial practices. In these communities, the deceased's body was properly attended to by family and friends; it would have been washed for burial probably by a family member or other individual with special training (as was the case in African society) and watched over at night prior to its burial in a day or two.[238]

In such places as North Kingstown and Newport, where a large Black community of free and enslaved people had endured for generations, the organizing of funerals was conducted by an "undertaker," a term more specific to the tasks of arranging the memorial service and burial of the deceased, most often in partnership with the church sexton.

Again, Knoblock noted that the practices of the enslaved were often similar to their masters: "For the enslaved and free alike in early New England, a proper African funeral service was considered important so that the deceased could live properly after death, a failure to do so meaning that the deceased might become a wandering ghost that could hurt or harm the living."[239]

The sprawling grounds of Updike's Cocumscussoc, better known for its mid-eighteenth-century Georgian manor house called Smith's Castle, held an indigenous burial ground at a site close by a cove and the mouth of what was then called Sawmill Creek in North Kingstown. Long known to locals, the burial site was used for the slaves who lived and worked the plantation for many years and may also have seen additional burials of indigenous people and domestic slaves from the community.

It was listed as the "burying point" on an 1802 survey and officially documented in 1883 by George Harris in his book *Anciente Burial Grounds of Olde Kingstowne*. Harris counted seventy-two large graves and eight smaller graves within the plot and speculated that there may have been other stones, which were removed. All of these were crude markers for the men, women and children who spent their lives working at Cocumscussoc and other farms. The number of graves alone would seem to indicate that the burial point was used for the burial of slaves belonging to neighboring families as well.

An old stone dock, merely referenced at the time of the Harris map as being built sometime before 1800, jutted out from the point to a deep channel. North Kingstown resident Harriet Spink Smith kept a near lifelong diary of happenings in the town, writing wistfully as she revisited the site in her older years:

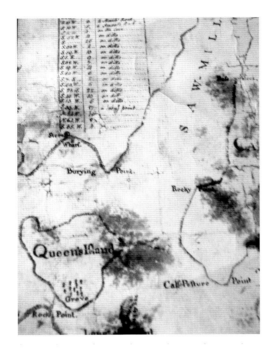

Map by William Harris detailing location of "Burial Point" at Cocumscussoc, 1805. *Courtesy of the Cocumscussoc Archives.*

Nov. 1888—The old Indian Burying Place, I crossed or passed once more. There must have been nearer 200 than 100 graves in the early days. But now it having been out "to the commons" so long, most of the rough stones broken down. "Tony, son of Tony and Amey Moffatt," aged 6 years, died in 1764, I think. His engraved head stone flat on ground.

This diary refers to what was likely one of the oldest slave burial grounds in Rhode Island, as the plantation was owned by the Smith/Updike family from 1651 to 1813. Just inland from the old burying point lie the Aryault-Updike and Congdon burial lots, both fenced in with iron rails and granite posts in the nineteenth century. A triangular stone, much repaired, is a marker for the grave of Richard Smith.

It is unknown if any of the nine enslaved men, children and one woman whom Richard Smith Jr. owned during his transitioning of the trading post to a working plantation are buried here. He'd manumitted them in his will, but certainly the slaves who died at Cocumscussoc during that time and through the next three generations of ownership would have been buried at this site.

The slave burial ground was leveled in the early twentieth century as the nearby Devil's Foot ledge was quarried for its granite. The state needed the granite brought to Newport for projects and had a road constructed to the site of the old dock, which it then improved and used to load the granite onto ships for transport.

A popular 1992 guide to graveyards of the town makes no mention of any existing or lost slave lots. A notation by Fitts, in his research for his 1995 thesis on the Narragansett Planters at Brown University, seems to be the first mention of the burial ground at Cocumscussoc since Harris's recording. Later publication of *Captive at Cocumscussoc* by former Cocumscussoc Association president Neil Dunay in 2016, provided a map and updated information about the site, as did this author in *A Cocumscussoc Reader* in 2017, in which several excerpts from Harriet Smith's journal mentioning the site were published.

Author Knoblock made no specific mention of the site but recorded a list of many others similarly lost as the slave burial ground at Cocumscussoc:

> *These include the Potter family slave lot in Cranston, four Gardner family slave or servant lots, the Morey family slave lot, and the "colored" lot on the Shatner Farm, all in Exeter; the Sambo lot, the Phillip's slave lot, the Willet-Carpenter lot, and three other designated slave lots in North Kingstown; the Babcock slave lot, the Dockray slave lot, and two general slave lots in South Kingstown; the Spink slave cemetery, the Waterman family slave lot, and the Peter Greene slave lot in Warwick; and the Thompson family slave lot in Westerly.*

Many of these slave lots were recorded to be in a run-down and overgrown condition by James N. Arnold and George J. Harris in the 1880s, as they compiled the first farm-by-farm survey of private cemeteries in the region. These were especially useful to the Rhode Island genealogical societies' efforts to update the status of these historic cemeteries in South Kingstown, Exeter, Westerly, Newport, Warwick and Providence.

Knoblock's referenced "Potter family slave lot" in Cranston may have lain near the Potter family plot (CR014) off Pippin Orchard Road in current-day Cranston, then part of Scituate, but it was more likely close by the homestead on Burndt Hill, the crest of a ridge that now lies within sight of the Scituate Reservoir. The slave lot would have lain on what was named Riverlet Farm and was likely lost to the plow generations ago.

Another slave lot belonging to slaves of the Baker family off Natick Avenue has also been lost. Harris located the Phillips slave lot on May 8, 1881, with his notation:

On land of John Smith southwest of his house on knoll without protection[,]
a burial yard of the colored servants of the Phillips family, the former owner
of the property....Here lyeth Lonnen negro servant of Christopher Phillips
who died Jan ye 24 1726/7 aged 22 years....Hagur sister of Lonnen
negro servant of Christopher Phillips died April ye 22 1727 aged 19 years.

South 2 graves with rude stones
Head S u North 1 grave same
At feet south 1 Large then 2 small then 2 large
"   " again 4 " same..."

This main stone for Lonnen and his sister was elaborate for a slave memorial and indicates they were likely domestic slaves. The stone itself was rescued from the plow, and by the late twentieth century, it had been preserved in the Stevens shop in Newport.

Long forgotten, amid the overgrown pastures of the old planter estates, were the lots where the enslaved who labored on the farms and in the kitchens of those houses were buried. Harris recorded the Willett-Carpenter slave lot "on a knoll a few rods south west from the [Carpenter Burial Ground] on opposite side of road in an open lot and unprotected is a burial yard containing 10 graves we are told were slaves of the Willet and Carpenter families. Whither there were more graves we know not though the plow has run fearfully close."[240] He added, "Probably others were here where stones have been removed and the graves obliterated."[241]

That same month, he located another lot at the "foot of Wolmesley hill east from northwest corner of road towards river beside wall in lot unprotected we find a burial yard containing 16 large and 9 small graves. We are told these are colored people who used to live in this vicinity."[242]

The Gardner family was extensive throughout the area we now call South County; nearly all were descendants of Squire Nicholas Gardner (1738–1815). The Gardner/Stanton slave burial ground (EX139), which originally lay on land in both North and South Kingstown, contained many of the graves of the family's former slaves. A description of the now lost burial plot written by Arnold in 1880 reads: "A short distance north of the old house...is a colored burial yard—graves that have no protection and marked with rude stones only. In this yard are buried two well-known old darkies, servants formerly of Squire Nicholas Gardner who gave them a horse on his decease."

It is unknown whether these two black men referred to were the former enslaved laborers who had served in the Revolutionary War, but in the years after the American victory, their service was often acknowledged in the communities where they lived and in the obituaries published after their deaths.[243]

Primus Gardner served as a private in Dexter's company. He died on October 20, 1780. Ruttee Gardner served in the regiment with Captain Lewis's company. He appears to have served out his time with the regiment and likely was injured or became ill during his time of service. He was listed as "sick in North Kingstown in March of 1779"[244] and discharged from service in April of that year. His illness or injuries seems to have continued to plague him, for on March 28, 1785, Hezekiah Babcock submitted a bill to the Town of Hopkington for the "boarding and nursing of Rutter Gardner, a negro man who formerly belonged to Nicholas Gardner of Exeter, and a late soldier in the Rhode Island Continental Regiment."[245] He may have been a relation of George and Thankful Gardner.

A slave of Ezekial Gardner Jr. (1738–1814) of North Kingstown also enlisted in the regiment. Gardner was an influential man in town and appointed to be the enlistment officer for the Continental army on June 28, 1775. A second man, Hercules Gardner, enlisted to earn his freedom and served in Captain Thomas Cole's company before being transferred to the "Corps of Invalids," a unit of soldiers recovering from illness or wounds and afforded light duty.

Another dozen slaves of other members of the Gardner family appear on the rolls of the regiment in the DAR publication of *Forgotten Patriots*. Whether for three months, or three years, each had served time in the cause to earn freedom, if not their own.

While seeking the Nathan Gardner lot (SK 114) in May 1880, Arnold found the family lot in good condition, but "west of the above, a few yards is a slave burial yard overgrown with weeds, briar, and birch so dense as to render a count of graves impossible." Arnold found another slave lot close by the Colonel Henry Gardiner lot off Stony Fort Road, on what was also known as the Samuel Stanton farm. Near a sawmill in the woods, he located "an extensive burial yard of the slaves of the Gardiner family." Though the plot was "overgrown with briars and weeds," he counted some seventy-five or eighty graves. This lot has been designated (NKHS 180).

The Polodor Gardner Lot lay east of what is now Ministerial Road (at telephone pole 170) on the west side of Long Pond Road and contained the graves of Thankful Gardner, her daughter Cornelia Franklin and son-in-law

John. Arnold described it as follows: "south of Mr. Franklin's house a burial yard, containing one grave (no marker) being that of Thankful Gardiner (colored) lot fenced and partly walled. About here we find several graves buried without much order being those of colored people"[246]

This cemetery was accidently unearthed during a private construction project in October 1998. It remains on private land.

Locating the George Babcock burial yard (SK 25) "marked by rude stones" east of Matunuck Beach in October 1880, Arnold also located close by "one grave that of a slave of the above named George Babcock named Plato Babcock."[247]

Arnold searched for the Babcock family slave lot on October 6, 1880, on "land owned by Mrs. Randall (now Tuckertown Park). It is said that north of their barn was an old slave burial ground which has disappeared, said to have been slaves of the Babcock family."

More veterans lay in these cemeteries. One of Hezekiah Babcock's slaves named Ceaser Babcock enlisted in the local militia in 1775 in his master's stead. He did the same in 1778 when the call came for more recruits. According to his pension application, "In the summer of that year was on the Island of Rhode Island where in an action with the enemy he saw a drummer by the name of Card killed by a shot in the breast while very near him."[248]

Babcock's application testified that he had seen nearly a year and a half of service, well past the six-month requirement to apply for a pension. As there was little documentation, however, his pension request was rejected. In response, two fellow soldiers from the regiment wrote to testify that they had served with Caeser. The minister of the Baptist church in Newport wrote to vouch for the two men who had written in support, "Being aware that the statements of 'negroes' we sometimes regard with a degree of suspicion." Martha Babcock wrote to the committee that "Ceaser was a slave to my said husband before the Revolutionary War and Ceaser served as a soldier in the militia for my said husband and went to the Island of Rhode Island with the army commanded by General Sullivan to act against the British."[249]

None of these could dissuade the committee, and he never received a pension. There was little recognition of his service until his name was included on the monument at Patriots Park.

Other enslaved men owned by the Babcocks who served in the First Rhode Island regiment included Primus Babcock, who enlisted in the regiment at the age of thirty-eight and served for the remainder of the war. He returned to Hopkington and used his skill as a cobbler to make a living.

These, and other graves of Black veterans of the Revolutionary War, were mostly left unmarked and unadorned with the wreath-enclosed, star-centered symbol we've grown accustomed to seeing before some of the oldest tombstones in our cemeteries.

By the time the DAR began marking Revolutionary War graves in the 1890s, many of the resting places of these slaves turned servants and laborers had already been neglected for decades. Largely for that reason, a monument to the men of color who served in the American Revolution was erected in Portsmouth, Rhode Island, within the site of the Battle of Rhode Island in which the First Rhode Island Regiment was engaged in the field for the first time.

The Robinson family plots, through four generations, lay at Canonchet Farm (NG 009) in Narragansett, another nearby on Ginger Lane (NG013) and a small plot that still remains by Rowland Robinson's house on the old Boston Neck Road. The latter Robinson especially was known to have had many slaves. Among them was Prince Robinson, who claimed to

The memorial to the "Black Regiment" at Patriots Park, Portsmouth, Rhode Island. *Photo by the author.*

be descended from royalty. He held great influence over the areas slave population for many years, being elected as "president" in the annual "black elections" that were a tradition in both northern and some southern slave communities. Prince made a living in his elder years selling apples and gingerbread to state representatives gathered for session near his home in Little Rest.[250]

A Hazard family plot also lies on Old Boston Neck Road (NK214), and there is another on Tower Hill Road (NK118). This family also held several generations of slaves, though the sites of their burials are now lost. As both families held large numbers of Quakers, their slaves may have been buried in Friend cemeteries in both North and South Kingstown.[251]

Others may have been interred in one of the "slave lots" or "Indian lots" identified on Stony Lane Road in what is presently Exeter, Rhode Island. As mentioned before, these were often adapted by local residents as slave lots, and just as often, the origins of the slaves and indentured servants who labored on farms and in private industry throughout South County were often blurred or misunderstood by the white inhabitants.

Daniel Stedman of South Kingstown, a farmer and shoemaker, was also an elder at the First Baptist Church. As such, he visited other church members routinely, sat watch before funerals and, on occasion, married local couples, including people of color. Stedman took his duties as an elder with a great sense of importance. He was a sharp-penned chronicler of the community and staunch believer in temperance, as displayed by his entry on April 28, 1827: "Died very sudden Pat Dimmis a colored person at the Widow Sweet's. Lay down in Liquor and went to Sleep and Never awoke." Dimmis's body apparently lay at the widow's house for over a week, waiting to be claimed. On May 8, Stedman noted, "The Indians took up Pat Dimmis and Carried her to Charlestown to Bury."[252]

The "servants lot" of the extended family of Captain Samuel Browning (1718–1764), who married Phebe Gardner (1722–1810) of that prominent family, still remains on the property today. The manor house and its extensive additions are still in fine condition. While the Browning plot was removed to Elm Grove Cemetery after 1880, the servants' and slaves' remains were left behind where they had been buried in a separate plot (NK132) off nearby Plantation Lane. The cemetery remains very well maintained, the stone wall enclosing the lot in good condition, seemingly as Arnold found it in 1880, writing that he found the lot in the "orchard southwest corner," where there lay "seven graves being those of colored people who used to live with the Browning family."

An "unknown lot" lying 90 feet southeast of the Robert Brown lot (SK 138) in what is now part of the great Swamp Wildlife Management Area was found in 2001 by Ranger Charles Allin, is believed to hold the graves of enslaved laborers, once marked by uninscribed fieldstones, of the Brown family.

The Dockray slave lot, according to Arnold's account, lay "on land of Edward H. Hazard north west of Old Dockray burial yard" (SK 69). It contained about twenty-five graves, but was protected by only one wall, and otherwise open to the elements. It is believed that it was located on Pine Hill or Woodbine Roads and was formerly listed as SK565.

Another lot off Old Pasaquiset trail in Charlestown likely contains the grave of Jacob Perry, a Black man who was listed in the town's 1850 census as being eighty-four. He was born in 1766, likely into a slave family.

One of the two "general lots" mentioned by Knoblock could be the "colored yard" that Arnold found "a short distance" from the John L. Brown lot at Bridgetown and the William H. Perry lots at the foot of Tower Hill near Middlebridge Road. This lot lay unprotected at the time, in the southern corner of a pasture lot. The slaves buried here were mentioned in Stedman's Journal as Dianna and George Perry. The Baptist elder recorded on April 2, 1852, "At Night Died Wife of Mr. George Perry (colored) at Wakefield with the Consumption. She left 2 Small Children, I am informed." Their son George G. Perry married Louisa Ann, daughter of London Weeden at South Kingstown on March 5, 1846.[253]

The other is likely the slave lot found on the property of the University of Rhode Island, when Arnold was searching for the George Tefft lot that once lay east of Plains Road on the campus. He found the slave burial yard "overgrown with bayberry and briars" but still in existence and filled "with rude stones. This is supposed to be those of slaves and there [is] another similar yard about the same distance further northeast on south side of stone wall now nearly obliterated by the plow."[254]

The Judge E.R. Potter paupers' plot likely contains slave burial sites as well, as it became a burial yard for inmates who were executed or died of suicide, as well as vagrants and poverty-stricken elderly of the community.

Another more "public" burial ground lay on South Road beside the "colored church" known as the Brown Chapel. On his visit on October 2, 1880, Arnold recorded, "In church yard of the colored church south of Curtis Corner, lot walled but in poor condition." He counted fifty-six markers, with but sixteen of them inscribed and the remaining thirty-seven plain fieldstones. By 1993, two marble stones, two crudely inscribed fieldstones and fourteen unmarked fieldstones were all that remained.

The former Browning Plantation, Saunderstown, Rhode Island. *Photo by the author.*

The "slave lot" on the property of the Browning Plantation. *Photo by the author.*

One grave of note is that of John White, who was born enslaved in Virginia and settled in Kingston, Rhode Island, after the Civil War. He worked long hours in the marble shop in the village and often told locals stories of his enslavement during his youth. After his death on July 15, 1895, he was placed in what is now known as the Old Fayerwether Cemetery, then the village burial ground beside the Baptist church.[255]

A number of enslaved persons were also buried in what was described as the "small pox lot," located on Cardinal Lane. Arnold's visit in 1880 found "a large number of graves buried without much order and marked with rude stones." These were the burial sites of victims of a smallpox epidemic around 1757. Arnold found forty-nine large and sixty-one small graves. The area is now heavily overgrown with briars, and researchers were later to locate only thirty to forty stones.

Newport's Common Burying Ground on Farewell Avenue holds the largest number of African American graves in the state. As we have seen, the city was a bustling commercial seaport during the colonial period, and many of the graves in "God's Little Acre" are those of the slaves of the merchants, or those of the many who were brought Newport to be apprentices in the shipbuilding industry as carpenters or rope makers, furniture craftsmen or stone masons.[256] A significant number of the historical structures still standing in Newport and other cities that date from colonial times were constructed in part by these craftsman and the labor of both enslaved and free African Americans.

Elsewhere in Rhode Island, the loss of private burial grounds has meant the loss of more slave lots on property once owned by prominent slaveholders. The Peter Greene slave lot once lay in close proximity to his grand colonial house by Narragansett Bay in Warwick, Rhode Island. The burial ground could be found off of Symonds Avenue (WK-123) before the lot was purchased and dug up for a swimming pool.

The Waterman family in Warwick, descended from Richard Waterman, one of the original proprietors of Providence, also held a substantial farm in the town. It was established in 1642 when John Waterman constructed a stone-ender on the site. The later colonial John Robinson Waterman house (1800), built when its owner was but seventeen, still stands today on the remaining acreage of the Lockwood Brook Farm on what was called "Old Homestead Drive" until it became Homestead Road.

The Federal-style two-and-a-half story house, with its paired chimneys and elegant doorway, was constructed by craftsmen from Newport with chestnut timbers, oak floorboards and bricks manufactured on the property.

The H-shaped house holds a central hall, with eight main rooms and a ballroom on the second floor. Each of the main rooms features a fireplace and is accessible from the hall, perfectly suited for a large family and the servants who catered to their needs.[257]

The lot registered as "Waterman Slaves" (WK 103) also lies on the property, with one remaining memorial. Among the known individuals enslaved by the family were Prince, Parmalee, Cuff and Flora Waterman. The oldest interred was known to be Cholie Waterman, who died at the age of ninety. An earlier lot was likely lost with the sale of land and development of housing in the mid-twentieth century. Such was the fate of many small lots that went unnoticed and were destroyed intentionally or by accident.

The burial place of the slaves of the Spink family of what was then Warwick remains on the private land of an industrial complex in what is now West Warwick. The lot contains the gravestones of Ceaser Spink, who died at seventy-eight, twenty-five-year-old William Spink and Vinah Spink, who also died young, at sixteen. The lot also includes markers for Lucy, Frances and Betty Spink. An individual named Lucy Rooms is also interred there.

By contrast to these family plots and slave lots among Rhode Island's rural areas, the loss of urban plots came early. Often, long neglected slave lots were dug up for building projects and reburied. Subsequent lots for the enslaved were laid out in the far-flung corners of common burial grounds.

In Providence's North Burial Ground, a cemetery that began as a common burying ground in the 1660s—adding the graves of indigent inhabitants to a corner of the land that had been an indigenous burial site—was still also used as a common for grazing cattle and sheep. It was formally declared a burial ground in 1700 and opened to all citizens from the prominent to the poor. With the popular effort in the mid-1800s to transform such burial grounds into landscaped parks, the North Burial Ground was also transformed into a place of beauty for those who wished to be interred in such a setting, but it also marked the creation of the distinct separation between the wealthy and middle class and poor with the creation of a "potter's field." It lies not just beyond those graves of the more prominent citizens but across a bridge traversing an abandoned stretch of canal on a thin strip of land below the lanes of a busy interstate highway.

In 1964, the colonial graves of some enslaved that had been allowed to remain where they had been originally interred were removed to give the state a slice of the cemetery land through which the newly constructed I-95 would pass. Stones were laid out face up, adjacent to the potter's field.

The monument to the enslaved laborers of the Waterman family. *Courtesy of the Rhode Island Historic Cemetery Commission.*

Here, the stones of Eve, the wife of Prince Cushing (1730–1780); Hannah Mar(s), who died a free woman in 1818; the small stone of two-year-old Primus Tillinghast (1748–1750); and the gravestone of Robert Millet, a slave from Fayetteville, North Carolina, who died in Providence on September 4, 1823, lie with some thirty-eight other stones exposed to the elements. A large granite monument acknowledges their removal from the cemetery grounds but contains none of the names carved on the disintegrating stones.

The Anglicization of slaves, especially those domestic slaves in urban settings, was particularly successful, at least from the enslavers' point of view. Faithfulness and longevity seemed to have counted a great deal as to whether or not an enslaved domestic worker was recognized with a memorial marker.

Two remaining gravestones of enslaved women from that period remain in the Newman Cemetery in East Providence. A Congregational cemetery long associated with the Newman Congregational Church, the burial ground is one of the oldest in the state, and as it lays in an area that was once part of Rehobeth, many of that town's early residents are interred in the older part of the cemetery.

The graves of two slaves lie close to each other, though they were owned by separate families; one suspects other slave and "colored" graves were once nearby. One this author particularly came to find was the gravestone of Anna Bowen, a long-lived slave of Colonel Jabez Bowen whose inscription, "Thou a good master, I was a good slave, I now rest from labor and sleep in my grave," was included in Marion Pearce Carter's *The Old Rehobeth Cemetery: The Ring Around Town*. Anna died "aged about 80 years."

Just feet away lies the grave of a domestic slave of John Hunt, another prominent citizen of East Providence, who established the early Hunt Mill along the Ten Mile River as it snaked through the town.

The inscription on her gravestone reads

In Memory of
SHERREY
The true and faithfull
Negro Servant
Of Mr. John Hunt
Who died Jul 31ˢᵗ
1762 Aged
about 80 years

There were exceptions to longevity, however: the small grave of two-year-old Primus Tillinghast (1748–1750), the son of a favored domestic slave, in the North Burial Ground, and likewise the elegantly carved gravestone of Bristol Bernan (1748–1762), the son of Hannah, a "servant" of Gideon Crawford in the same cemetery.

The DeWolf family in Bristol also included a lifelong slave of the household, Adjua DeWolf (1794–1868), who, tradition has it, was brought with a young boy named Pauledore directly from Africa as a pair of Christmas presents for Nancy DeWolf in 1803. The pair later married and became fixtures in Bristol. They had a cabin on the property and remained popular domestic servants until their old age, though Adjua's marker is the only carved gravestone among the others in a section at the edge of a wooded lot that borders the cemetery.

Perhaps the most remarkable remembrance in stone of a domestic slave can be found in the elegant Swan Point cemetery of Providence, where the side of a hill holds an elegant memorial, a narrow slate stone from an earlier era, on which is carved:

Walker, a native of the Sandwich Islands
brought from Owhu by B.D. Jones in August 1804,
died in 1814, being about 18 years
He was a faithful and affectionate servant

Above: Potter's Field in Providence's North Burial Ground. *Photo by the author*.

Left: The gravestone of "Sherry," Newman Cemetery, East Providence, Rhode Island. *Photo by the author*.

This means that despite Rhode Island's ban on the importation of slaves, Jones, like other merchants and slave traders of the period, found ways to circumnavigate the law. A highly successful merchant with at least one vessel at his disposal, Jones may have registered the enslaved child as a "cabin boy" but effectively secured him for his "house boy" or personal slave at home.

It also illustrates that this was a slave held in true affection by the family, for Walker was the exception from most family slave. His stone, if not his remains, was moved with the family plot nearly thirty years after his death. It is one of the few memorials to an enslaved person that was not left behind to be forgotten.

The gravestone of "Walker," Swan Point Cemetery, Providence, Rhode Island. *Photo by the author.*

NOTES

Prologue

1. Eric Kimball, "What Have We to Do With Slavery?: New Englanders and the Slave Economics of the West Indies," in Beckert and Rockman, *Slavery's Capitalism*, 183.
2. Ibid.
3. Bridenbaugh and Bridenbaugh, *No Peace Beyond the Line*, 94.
4. As quoted in Warren's *God, War, and Providence*, 72, citing Winthrop's journal, vol. 1, p. 132.
5. Rhode Island Historical Society, Robinson Research Library [hereafter RIHS], MSS 770 Case 2, item 57.
6. Daniels, *Dissent and Conformity*, 17.
7. Lippincott, *Indians, Privateers and High Society*, 45.
8. Daniels, *Dissent and Conformity*, 18.
9. Ibid.
10. Lippincott, *Indians, Privateers and High Society*, 45.

Chapter 1

11. Beckert and Rockman, *Slavery's Capitalism*, 183.
12. Ibid.
13. Dunn, *Sugar and Slaves*, 15.
14. Ibid., 23.
15. Richard B. Sheridan, "The Domestic Economy," in Greene, *Colonial British America*, 50–51.

16. Morgan, *American Slavery*, 303.
17. Hubbard, *General History*, 532.
18. Russell, *Long, Deep Furrow*, 164–65.
19. Ibid., 123.
20. Ibid.
21. Ibid.
22. Brandow, *Genealogies of Barbados Families*, 663.
23. Hubbard, *General History*, 518.
24. Brandow, *Genealogies of Barbados Families*, 667.
25. Ibid., 670.
26. Ibid., 245.
27. Bridenbaugh, *Fat Mutton*, 117.
28. Russell, *Long, Deep Furrow*, 156.
29. Dunn, *Sugar and Slaves*, 34–35.
30. Pares, *Yankees and Creoles*, 111.
31. Adams, *Commerce of Rhode Island*, vol. 1, 1.
32. Ibid., 11.
33. Ibid., 15.
34. Coughtry, *Notorious Triangle*, 241–85.
35. Pares, *Yankess and Creoles*, 2–3.
36. Updike, *Richard Smith*, 20.
37. Bailyn, *New England Merchants*, 59.
38. Ibid., 58.
39. Ibid., 95.
40. John Chace married Ann Arnold, daughter of Benedict Arnold, in 1713. He died in Newport in 1745.
41. Updike, *History of the Narragansett Church*, 418.
42. John Carter Brown Library Archive of Early American Images, No. 8189-32, *A New Map of Barbados*.
43. Neil Dunay, "Captive at Cocumscussoc: From Bondage to Freedom" in Cranston, *We Were Here Too*,
44. Fitts, "Inventing New England's Slave Paradise," 100.
45. Cranston, *We Were Here Too*, 91–92.
46. Kimball, "What Have We to Do With Slavery?"
47. McBurney, "South Kingstown Planters."
48. Ibid. McBurney's extensive, three-hundred-page treatment on the Narragansett planters, from which this article was taken, must be considered the foundation from which later modern scholars have begun their research, including a number whose works are referred to in this history.
49. Geake, *Historic Rhode Island Farms*, 81.
50. McBurney, "South Kingstown Planters," 7.

51. Updike, *History of the Narragansett Church*, 515–17. Though this use of the South Ferry has been disputed, further evidence may lie in the few sales between Robinson and Lopez for livestock, one of which included two oxen in 1772, perhaps indicating that Robinson's sloops were large enough for horses, hogs and sheep but larger livestock would be better sold to Lopez, who often shipped such goods on his brigantines.

52. Miller, *Narragansett Planters*, 22. See also Updike, *History of the Narragansett Church*, 515.

53. Fitts, "Inventing New England's Slave Paradise," 100.

54. Bailyn, *New England Merchants*, 55.

55. Slavery in the North, http://slavenorth.com/connecticut.htm.

56. Russell, *Long, Deep Furrow*, 162.

57. Ibid.

58. Now known as Newport.

59. Hedges, *Browns of Providence Plantations*, 4–5.

60. Browne, *Letter Book of James Browne*.

61. Griggs, *Early Homesteads*, 5, 6.

62. Ibid.

63. Hedges, *Browns of Providence Plantations*, 5.

64. Pares, *Yankees and Creoles*, 37n.

65. Russell, *Long, Deep Furrow*, 143.

66. Ibid., 38.

67. Ibid., 37.

68. For a detailed account of the Browns' production of these candles, see this author's *History of the Providence River*, 63–65.

69. Main, *Society and Economy*, 222.

70. *Hartford Courant*, "The Plantation Next Door," September 29, 2002

71. Coleman, *Transformation of Rhode Island*, 45.

Chapter 2

72. Kimball, "What Have We to Do With Slavery?," 181

73. From a presentation by Prof. Linford Fisher, titled "'Fetcht from other Countries': Indian Slavery in the English Atlantic," which was given at the John Carter Brown Library Seminar in the History of the Americas and the World, April 15, 2015.

74. Ibid.

75. Ibid., 18.

76. Dunn and Yeadle, *Journal of John Winthrop*. See also Warren, *New England Bound*, 37.

77. Dunn and Yeadle, *Journal of John Winthrop*.

78. Ibid., 95.

79. Newell, *Brethren by Nature*, 154.
80. Nathaniel Saltonstall, "The Present State of New England," in *Narratives of the Indian Wars*, 57.
81. Newell, *Brethren by Nature*, 152.
82. Morgan, *American Slavery*, 301.
83. Greene, *Negro in Colonial New England*, 16–17.
84. Ibid., 32.
85. Ibid. This prevalence of boy slaves refers to a preference of the wealthy to young, and therefore more controllable and docile slaves in one's household. Boys tended to become personal servants to masters.
86. Winsor, *Memorial History of Boston*, vol. 2, 262–63 In respect to the previous note, some recent articles have used this letter and the name of his ship to imply that the younger Faneuil was homosexual. More likely, wealthy urban professionals and urban planters alike seemed to have had a preference for young males to serve as valets in their mansion houses.
87. As quoted in Greene, *Negro in Colonial New England*, 28. Attributed to the *Dictionary of American Biography*, vol. 19, 333.
88. Weeden, *Early Rhode Island*, 187.
89. Coleman, *Transformation of Rhode Island*, 32.
90. Crane, *Dependent People*, 31.
91. Coughtry, *Notorious Triangle*, 253.
92. Adams, *Commerce of Rhode Island*, vol. 1., 217, 224, 230.
93. Crane, *Dependent People*, 26.
94. Ibid., 55.
95. The pink sandstone mansion burned on June 7, 1766. So famous were the grounds of the estate that in 1796 an effort was made to establish an arboretum and charge public admission, much as the neighboring preserved mansions do now. The existing stone dwelling, much amended over the years was constructed in 1849. See http://historic-structures.com/ri/newport/malbone.php.
96. RIHS, MSS 549, vol. 1 Malbone Account Book 1728–1738, 22.
97. Ibid., 50.
98. Crane, *Dependent People*, 69.
99. Ibid., 84.
100. *Hartford Courant*, "The Plantation Next Door," September 29, 2002.
101. As quoted in Rackove, *Revolutionaries*, 7.
102. *Newport Mercury*, June 6, 1763.
103. Pares, *Yankees and Creoles*, 100.
104. Coughtry, *Notorious Triangle*, 72.
105. RIHS, MSS 541, folder 3, logbook of Nathaniel Briggs.
106. Wolf, *As Various as Their Land*, 169.
107. RIHS, MSS 541, folder 3, logbook of Nathaniel Briggs.

108. Anamaboe Road refers to the slave traffic that occurred from the string of forts in the shadow of Cape Coast Castle on the Gold Coast of Africa. At the peak of the slave-buying season, ships lined up offshore and had slaves rowed to them by the hundreds each day.
109. Ibid.
110. Majory O'Toole, "Slave Traders," Little Compton Historical Society, http://littlecompton.org, June 18, 2016.
111. *Bulletin of the Newport Historical Society*, no. 75A, December 3, 2013 .
112. Newport Historical Society Collection, Peleg Clarke Letter-Book, 76.
113. Coughtry, *Notorious Triangle*, 50.
114. Lippincott, *Indians, Privateers and High Society*.
115. Sparks, *Where the Negroes Are Masters*, 165.
116. Ibid., 125.
117. Ibid., 126.
118. Ibid., 129.
119. Ibid.
120. Crane, *Dependent People*, 24.
121. Sparks, *Where the Negroes Are Masters*, 80.
122. Desrosiers, *John Bannister of Newport*, 184–86.
123. RIHS, MSS 119, John Bannister Account Books, ledger B, 331.
124. Ibid., 101.
125. As quoted in Geake, *History of the Providence River*, 42.
126. Coleman, *Transformation of Rhode Island*, 55.
127. Ibid., 56.
128. See "Slavery in Connecticut," Slavery in the North, http://slavenorth.com/connecticut.htm.
129. Ibid.
130. Main, *Society and Economy in Colonial Connecticut*, 176–78.
131. Greene, *Negro in Colonial New England*, 98–99.
132. See *Hartford Courant*, "Connecticut Slave Owners in 1790," September 29, 2002. The listing in the *Courant*'s article is taken from research conducted by Goucun Yang for his doctoral dissertation, "From Slavery to Emancipation: The African Americans of Connecticut 1650s–1820s" (University of Connecticut, 1999).
133. Society of Middletown First Settler Descendants, middletown1650.org.
134. Hesselberg, "Vanished Port."
135. Ibid., 10.
136. Ibid.
137. Farrow, Lang and Frank, *Complicity*, 115.
138. Farrow, *Logbooks*, 1–2.
139. Main, *Society and Economy in Colonial Connecticut*, 259–60.
140. As quoted in Hesselberg, "Vanished Port," 11

141. Adams, *Commerce of Rhode Island*, vol. 2, 443–44.

142. RIHS, MSS 333, SGI Series 1, B9, F4 Subseries 1 List/Letter to Edward Carrington from William Lees.

143. Ibid.

144. Ibid., letter from Benjamin Hoppin, June 17, 1806.

145. Ibid., letter to Edward Carrington from Benjamin Hoppin, June 4, 1807.

146. Stephen Chambers, "No Country but Their Counting Houses," in Beckert and Rockman, *Slavery's Capitalism*, 198.

147. Wolf, *As Various as Their Land*, 52.

148. Sharon Cummins, "Mainers Engaged in the Slave Trade in the 1800s," Seacoastonline.com.

149. Smith, *Memoirs*, 23–24.

150. Ibid., 26.

151. Ibid., 27.

152. Ibid., 28.

153. Coleman, *Transformation of Rhode Island*, 46.

Chapter 3

154. Strensrud, *Newport*, 298–99.

155. Adams, *Commerce of Rhode Island*, vol. 1, 44.

156. Ibid., 134.

157. Ibid., 150.

158. Russell, *Long, Deep Furrow*, 372.

159. Ibid. 340

160. Coleman, *Transformation of Rhode Island*, 32.

161. *Commerce in Rhode Island*, vol. 1., 377.

162. Geake, *Historic Rhode Island Farms*, 25.

163. Coleman, *Transformation of Rhode Island*, 32.

164. Coughtry, *Notorious Triangle*, 172.

165. *Commerce in Rhode Island*, vol. 1, 60.

166. *Commerce in Rhode Island*, vol. 2, 242.

167. Ibid., 243.

168. Ibid., 359.

169. Fitts, "Inventing New England's Slave Paradise," 103. See also Washington County Supreme Court Records.

170. RIHS MSS 828, Box 12, folder 2, logbooks of the *Dolphin*, *Rising Sun* and *Fame*.

171. Ibid.

172. Ibid.

173. Coughtry, *Notorious Triangle*, 263,

174. Crane, *Dependent People*, 162.

175. Preservation Society of Rhode Island, *Warren, Rhode Island: Statewide Preservation Report*, 1975.
176. Farrow, Lang and Frank, *Complicity*, 56–58.
177. Ibid., 59.
178. Coughtry, *Notorious Triangle*, 175.
179. Franklin and Schweninger, *In Search of the Promised Land*, 49
180. Ibid.

Chapter 4

181. Coleman, *Transformation of Rhode Island*, 107.
182. RIHS, MSS 254, Series 1, Zachariah Allen letter to James Aborn, Providence, November 8, 1809.
183. Clark-Pujara, *Dark Work*, 90.
184. RIHS, MSS 483, Series 1, Folder 2, correspondence of I.P. Hazard, Hazard Family Papers.
185. Ibid.
186. Shaw, "Slave Cloth."
187. Farrow, Lang and Frank, *Complicity*, 14.
188. RIHS, MSS 70, Updike Papers.
189. McBurney, *History of North Kingstown*, 182.
190. RIHS, MSS 629, box 1, folder 4, Davis Family Papers, Account Book.
191. RIHS, MSS 629, box 1, folder 5, Correspondence 1837–1841.
192. McBurney, *History of North Kingstown*, 181–82.
193. RIHS, MSS 71, box 5, folder 12, Letter Book, 1795–1807 including sloop *Providence* accounts.
194. RIHS, MSS 71, William Arnold Papers.
195. RIHS, letter from Richard James Arnold to S.A. Nales, Esq., 1834, in the Arnold and Screven Family Papers, 3419.
196. Hoffman and Hoffman, *North by South*.
197. Arnold and Screven Family Papers, 1762–1903.
198. Hoffman and Hoffman, *North by South*, 9.
199. Ibid., 42.
200. South Carolina Plantations, http: http://south-carolina-plantations.com/georgetown/weehaw.html.
201. Hal Brown, "James Utter Arnold, Entrepreneur of Warwick," unpublished biographical sketch, RIHS.
202. *New York Genealogical and Biographical Record*, 380.
203. RIHS, MSS 538, Lippitt Family Papers,
204. RIHS, MSS 538, series 4, book 1, folder 9, journal of the ship *Factor*.
205. Lippitt papers.

206. *Biographical Cyclopedia of Representative Men*, issue 589, 282, Google books.
207. Account book, F&S.W. Greene, 1808–1813, private collection.
208. Correspondence of William P. Greene, Day Books, 1808–1819, private collection.
209. Ibid.
210. Shaw, "Slave Cloth."
211. Inskeep, *Imperfect Union*, xxvii.
212. Rosenburg, *Life and Times*, 4.
213. Sumner would pay heavily for his stance on the abolition of slavery when on May 22, 1856, he was brutally beaten by the cane-wielding senator from South Carolina, Preston S. Brooks, the southerner's ire raised by a fiery speech Sumner had given two days before.
214. See Henry Louis Gates Jr. "Why Was Cotton 'King'?" PBS, *The African Americans: Many Rivers to Cross*, https://www.pbs.org/wnet/african-americans-many-rivers-to-cross/history/why-was-cotton-king.
215. Ibid.
216. "Decline and Recovery—Lowell National Historical Park," National Park Service, www.nps.gov/lowe/learn/photosmultimedia/decline.htm.

Chapter 5

217. Carbone, *Nathanael Greene*, 216.
218. Ibid., 229.
219. Ibid., 230.
220. Stegeman and Stegeman, *Caty*, 132.
221. Yale University Library, letter from Whitney to his father dated September 11, 1793, Whitney Papers.
222. Stegeman and Stegeman, *Caty*, 169.
223. RIHS, MSS 254, series 7, box 8, folder 5, Eliza Allen journal, Zachariah Allen Papers.
224. Ibid.
225. Hoffman and Hoffman, *North by South*, 234.

Chapter 6

226. Foner, *Short History of Reconstruction*, 99.
227. Ibid., 165.
228. Ibid., 170.
229. Larkin, *Reshaping of Everyday Life*, 19.
230. Ibid.

231. Foner, *Short History of Reconstruction*, 178.

232. Ibid., 227.

233. Hoffman and Hoffman, *North by South*, 267.

Chapter 7

234. No George Coggeshall appears on the Newport or Washington Count census of 1774, so we may assume that George was one of the slaves of the extensive Coggeshall family of Newport. The town census showed Nathanial Coggeshall owning nine slaves, Billings Coggeshall owning six, as well as four owned by James Coggeshall and three by Elisha Coggeshall.

235. Hazard, *Nailer Tom's Diary*, 3.

236. O'Toole, "Slave Traders."

237. Dunay, "Captive at Cocumscusssoc," in *We Were Here Too*, 83.

238. Knoblock, *African American Historic Burial Grounds*, 65.

239. Ibid., 69.

240. RIHS, George J. Harris, *A Visitation to the Cemeteries of Ancient Kingstowne*, vol. 1, *North Kingstown*, 47. This work may be found in the Robinson Research Library.

241. Ibid., 230.

242. Ibid., 49.

243. Geake and Spears, *From Slaves to Soldiers*, 118–20.

244. Grundset, *Forgotten Patriots*, 215.

245. Hopkington Town Probate Records TC 2:156.

246. Rhode Island Genealogical Society, *North Kingstown Historical Cemeteries*, 482. See also *Providence Journal*, November 22, 1998, Section C.

247. Rhode Island Genealogical Society *South Kingstown Historical Cemeteries*, 501.

248. Pension Application 339, National Archives.

249. Crowder, *African Americans and American Indians*, 16–17.

250. McBurney, *Kingston*, 89.

251. Bamberg, *Daniel Stedman's Journal*. Note Stedman's entry of February 28, 1857, "Died Caty Carpenter, Colored, at Stephen A. Robinsons Buried 2nd day of March at the Friends meeting House yard, Backside."

252. Bamberg, *Daniel Stedman's Journal*, 24.

253. Arnold, *Vital Records*, vol. 5, 2–26

254. Rhode Island Genealogical Society, *North Kingstown Historical Cemeteries*, 499.

255. McBurney, *History of North Kingstown*, 140.

256. Preservation Society of Newport, "God's Little Acre," http://newportmansions. org.

257. D'Amato and Spencer, "John R. Waterman House/Lockwood Brook Farm Part 1."

BIBLIOGRAPHY

Adams, Charles Francis, ed. *Commerce of Rhode Island 1726–1800*. 2 vols. Boston: Massachusetts Historical Society, 1914.

Arnold, James N. *Vital Records of Rhode Island*. Vol. 5. Providence, RI: Narrangansett Historical Publishing Company, 1907.

Bailyn, Bernard. *The New England Merchants in the Seventeenth Century*. Cambridge, MA: Harvard University Press, 1979.

Bamberg, Cherry Fletcher, ed. *Daniel Steadman's Journal, 1829–1859*. Providence: Rhode Island Genealogical Society, 2003.

Beckert, Sven, and Seth Rockman, eds. *Slavery's Capitalism: A New History of American Economic Development*. Philadelphia: University of Pennsylvania Press, 2016.

Berlin, Ira. *Many Thousands Gone: The First Two Centuries of Slavery in North America*. Cambridge, MA: Belknap/Harvard University Press, 1998.

Brandow, James C. *Genealogies of Barbados Families from Caribbeana and the Journal of Barbados Museum and Historical Society*. Baltimore: Clearfield Publishing, 2001.

Bridenbaugh, Carl. *Fat Mutton and Liberty of Conscience*. Providence, RI: Brown University Press, 1974.

Bridenbaugh, Carl, and Roberta Bridenbaugh. *No Peace Beyond the Line: The English in the Caribbean, 1624–1690*. New York: Oxford University Press, 1972.

Browne, James. *The Letter Book of James Browne of Providence, Merchant 1735–1738*. Vol. 1. Providence, RI: Historical Society, 1929.

Carbone, Gerald M. *Nathanael Greene: A Biography of the American Revolution*. New York: Palgrave Macmilian, 2008.

Clark-Pujara, Christy. *Dark Work: The Business of Slavery in Rhode Island*. New York: New York University Press, 2016.

Coleman, Peter J. *The Transformation of Rhode Island, 1790–1860*. Providence, RI: Brown University Press, 1963.

Coughtry, Jay. *The Notorious Triangle: Rhode Island in the African Slave Trade, 1700–1807*. Philadelphia: Temple University Press, 1981.

Crane, Elaine Foreman. *A Dependent People: Newport, Rhode Island in the Revolutionary Era*. New York: Fordham University Press, 1983.

Cranston, G. Timothy, with Neil Dunay. *We Were Here Too: Selected Stories of Black History in North Kingstown*. N.p.: CreateSpace, 2016.

Crowder, Jack Darrell. *African Americans and American Indians in the Revolutionary War*. Jefferson, NC: McFarland & Co., 2019.

D'Amato, Don, and Terry Spencer. "John R. Waterman House/Lockwood Brook Farm Part 1." *Warwick Beacon*, March 29, 2012

Daniels, Bruce C. *Dissent and Conformity on Narragansett Bay: The Colonial Rhode Island Town*. Middletown, CT: Wesleyan University Press, 1983.

Desrosiers, Marian Mathison. *John Bannister of Newport: The Life and Accounts of a Colonial Merchant*. Jefferson, NC: McFarland & Co., 2017.

Dunn, Richard S. *Sugar and Slaves: The Rise of the Planter Class in the British West Indies, 1624–1713*. Chapel Hill: University of North Carolina Press, 1972.

Dunn, Richard S., and Laetitia Yeadle, eds. *The Journal of John Winthrop*.

Farrow, Anne. *The Logbooks: Connecticut's Slave Ships and Human Memory*. Middletown, CT: Wesleyan University Press 2014

Farrow, Anne, Joel Lang and Jenifer Frank. *Complicity: How the North Promoted, Prolonged and Profited from Slavery*. New York: Ballantine Press, 2005.

Fisher, Linford. "'Fetcht from Other Countries': Indian Slavery in the English Atlantic." Paper given at a John Carter Brown Library Seminar on the History of the Americas and the World, April 15, 2015.

Fitts, Robert K. "Inventing New England's Slave Paradise: Master/Slave Relations in Eighteenth-Century Narragansett, Rhode Island." PhD diss., Brown University, 1995.

Foner, Eric. *A Short History of Reconstruction*. New York: Harper Perennial Modern Classics, 1988.

Franklin, John Hope, and Loren Schweninger. *In Search of the Promised Land: A Slave Family in the Old South*. New York: Oxford University Press, 2006.

Geake, Robert A. *Historic Rhode Island Farms*. Charleston, SC: The History Press, 2013.
———. *A History of the Providence River*. Charleston, SC: The History Press, 2014.

Geake, Robert A., and Lorén Spears. *From Slaves to Soldiers: The 1st Rhode Island Regiment in the Revolutionary War*. Yardley, PA: Westholme, 2016.

Gould, Philip. *Barbaric Traffic: Commerce and Antislavery in the 18th Century Atlantic World*. Cambridge, MA: Harvard University Press, 2003.

Greene, Jack, ed. *Colonial British America: Essays in the New History of the Early Modern Era*. Baltimore: Johns Hopkins University Press, 1984.

Greene, Lorenzo J. *The Negro in Colonial New England, 1620–1776*. New York: Columbia University Press, 1942.

Griggs, Susan J. *Early Homesteads of Pomfret and Hampton*. Danielson, CT: Ingalls Printing, 1950.

Grundset, Eric G., ed. *Forgotten Patriots: African and American Indian Patriots in the Revolutionary War*. Washington, D.C.: National Society of Daughters of the American Revolution, 2008.

Hazard, Caroline, ed. *Nailer Tom's Diary: Otherwise the Journal of Thomas B. Hazard of Kingstown, Rhode Island 1778–1840*. Boston: Merrymount Press, 1930.

Hedges, James B. *The Browns of Providence Plantations*. Cambridge, MA: Harvard University Press, 1956.

Hesselberg, Erik. "Vanished Port: Middletown and the Great Era of West Indies Tade." *Wesleyan University Magazine*, January 15, 2011.

Hoffman, Charles, and Tess Hoffman. *North by South: The Two Lives of Richard James Arnold*. Athens: University of Georgia Press, 2009.

Hubbard, William. *A General History of New England*. Boston: Massachusetts Historical Society, 1815.

Inskeep, Steve. *Imperfect Union: How Jesse and John Fremont Mapped the West, Invented Celebrity and Helped Cause the Civil War*. New York: Penguin Press, 2020.

Knoblock, Glenn A. *African American Historic Burial Grounds and Gravesites of New England*. Jefferson, NC: McFarland & Co., 2016.

Larkin, Jack. *The Reshaping of Everyday Life, 1790–1840*. New York: Harper & Row, 1988.

Lincoln, Charles Henry, John Easton, Nathaniel Saltonstal, Richard Hutchinson, Mary Wise Rowlandson and Cotton Mather. *Narratives of the Indian Wars, 1675–1699*. New York: Scribner's Sons, 1913.

Lippincott, William. *Indians, Privateers and High Society: A Rhode Island Sampler*. Philadelphia: J.B. Lippincott, 1961.

Main, Jackson Turner. *Society and Economy in Colonial Connecticut*. Princeton, NJ: Princeton University Press, 1985.

McBurney, Christian. *A History of North Kingstown, Rhode Island, 1700–1900*. Kingston, RI: Pettaquamscutt Historical Society, 2004.

———. *Kingston: A Forgotten History*. Kingston, RI: Pettaquamscutt Historical Society, 1975.

———. "The South Kingstown Planters: Country Gentry in Colonial Rhode Island." *Rhode Island Historical Society Bulletin*, August 1986.

Miller, William Davis. *The Narragansett Planters*. Worcester, MA: American Antiquarian Society, 1934.

Morgan, Edmund S. *American Slavery, American Freedom: The Ordeal of Colonial Virginia*. New York: Norton, 1975.

Newell, Margaret Ellen. *Brethren by Nature: New England Indians, Colonists, and the Origins of American Slavery*. Ithaca, NY: Cornell University Press, 2015.

The New York Genealogical and Biographical Record. Vol. 49. New York: New York Genealogical and Biographical Society, 1918.

Pares, Richard. *Yankees and Creoles: The Trade Between North America and the West Indies before the American Revolution.* Cambridge, MA: Harvard University Press, 1956.

Rackove, Jack. *Revolutionaries: A New History of the Invention of America.* Boston: Houghton-Mifflin Harcourt, 2010.

Rhode Island Genealogical Society. North Kingstown Historical Cemeteries. Salt Lake City, UT: Genealogical Society of Utah, 1973.

Rosenburg, Chaim M. *The Life and Times of Francis Cabot Lowell.* Lanham, MD: Lexington Books, 2011.

Russell, Howard S. *A Long, Deep Furrow: Three Centuries of Farming in New England.* Hanover, NH: University of New England Press, 1976.

Shaw, Madelyn. "Slave Cloth and Clothing Slaves: Craftsmanship, Commerce, and Industry." *Bulletin of the Museum of Southern Decorative Arts*, 2012.

Smith, Samuel. *Memoirs: A Soldier of the Revolution.* New York: Charles Bushnell, 1868.

Sparks, Randy J. *Where the Negroes Are Masters: An African Port in the Era of the Slave Trade.* Cambridge, MA: Harvard University Press, 2014.

Stegeman, John F. and Janet A. Stegeman. *Caty: A Biography of Catharine Littlefield Greene.* Providence: Rhode Island Bicentennial Foundation, 1977.

Strensrud, Rockwell. *Newport, A Lively Experiment, 1639–1969.* Newport, RI: Redwood Library, 2006.

Updike, Daniel Berkeley. *Richard Smith: First English Settler of the Narragansett County, Rhode Island.* Boston, Merrymount Press, 1937.

Updike, Wilkins. *A History of the Narragansett Church.* Boston: Merrymount Press, 1907.

Warren, James A. *God, War, and Providence.* Scribner, 2018.

Warren, Wendy. *New England Bound: Slavery and Colonization in Early America.* New York: Norton & Company, 2016.

Weeden, William B. *Early Rhode Island: A Social History of the People.* Grafton Press, 1910.

Winsor, Justin. *The Memorial History of Boston, 1630–1880.* Vol. 2. Boston, 1880

Wolf, Stephanie Grauman. *As Various as Their Land: The Everyday Lives of Eighteenth-Century Americans.* New York: Harper Collins, 1993.

INDEX

ABOUT THE AUTHOR

Robert A. Geake is a public historian who has written about Rhode Island and New England's history since he was seventeen and submitting stories for the local newspaper in Coventry, Rhode Island. He is the author of fourteen books, including *Keepers of the Bay: A History of the Narragansett Tribe, Native and New Americans, The New England Mariner Tradition, Colonial Curiosities, From Slaves to Soldiers: The 1ˢᵗ Rhode Island Regiment in the Revolutionary War* and *New England's Citizen Soldiers: Mariners and Minutemen.*

The author pictured with the slave medallion erected at Smith's Castle, North Kingstown, Rhode Island. *Photo by Charles Roberts.*

Mr. Geake currently serves as president of the Cocumscussoc Association, which runs Smith's Castle Historic House Museum, is a guide for Historic New England's Rhode Island sites, and also a reenactor with the Second Rhode Island Regiment. He is a member of the Association of Rhode Island Authors, the Rhode Island Historical Society and the John Carter Brown Library at Brown University.